SERIES

(ex·ploring)

1. Investigating in a systematic way: examining. 2. Searching into or ranging over for the purpose of discovery.

Getting Started with

Discipline Specific Projects

Series Editor Mary Anne Poatsy

Gionfriddo | Hogan | Lawson | Nowakowski

Series Created by Dr. Robert T. Grauer

Pearson

330 Hudson Street, NY, NY 10013

Vice President of IT & Career Skills: Andrew Gilfillan
Senior Portfolio Manager: Samantha Lewis
Team Lead, Project Management: Laura Burgess
Project Manager: Barbara Stover
Development Editor: Barbara Stover
Editorial Assistant: Michael Campbell
Director of Product Marketing: Maggie Waples
Director of Field Marketing: Leigh Ann Sims
Product Marketing Manager: Kaylee Carlson
Field Marketing Managers: Molly Schmidt & Joanna Conley
Senior Operations Specialist: Maura Zaldivar-Garcia
Interior and Cover Design: Cenveo
Senior Product Model Manager: Eric Hakanson
Production and Digital Studio Lead: Heather Darby
Media Producer, MyITLab: Jaimie Noy
Course Producer, MyITLab: Amanda Losonsky
Digital Project Manager, MyITLab: Becca Lowe
Media Project Manager, Production: John Cassar
Full-Service Project Management: Amy Kopperude, iEnergizer Aptara, Ltd.
Composition: iEnergizer Aptara, Ltd.
Cover Image Credits: cunico/Fotolia (*compass rose*); mawrhis/Fotolia (*checker pattern*); wavebreakmedia/Shutterstock (*students*); Sergey Nivens/Fotolia (*world*); dotshock/Shutterstock (*business people*)

Credits and acknowledgments borrowed from other sources and reproduced, with permission, in this textbook appear on the appropriate page within text.

Library of Congress Control Number on File

1 16

Pearson

ISBN 10: 0-13-449761-9
ISBN 13: 978-0-13-449761-7

Dedications

For my husband, Ted, who unselfishly continues to take on more than his share to support me throughout the process; and for my children, Laura, Carolyn, and Teddy, whose encouragement and love have been inspiring.

Mary Anne Poatsy

To my husband, Paul, and my children, Michael, Diana, and Robert, who have tried to be patient and understanding while I worked away on these projects. Thank you for your love, support, and encouragement.

Sheila Giofriddo

I dedicate this work to my wonderful family—my husband, Paul, and my daughters, Jenn and Alli. You have made this adventure possible with your support, encouragement, and love. You inspire me!

Lynn Hogan

This book is dedicated to my children and to my students to inspire them to never give up and to always keep reaching for their dreams.

Rebecca Lawson

To my wife, Jackie, for her patience when I have over-involved myself in supplements authoring.

Anthony Nowakowski

About the Authors

Mary Anne Poatsy, Series Editor

Mary Anne is a senior faculty member at Montgomery County Community College, teaching various computer application and concepts courses in face-to-face and online environments. She holds a B.A. in Psychology and Education from Mount Holyoke College and an M.B.A. in Finance from Northwestern University's Kellogg Graduate School of Management.

Mary Anne has more than 18 years of educational experience. She is currently adjunct faculty at Montgomery County Community College. She has also taught at Gywnedd Mercy University, Bucks County Community College, and Muhlenberg College, as well as conducted personal training. Before teaching, she was Vice President at Shearson Lehman in the Municipal Bond Investment Banking Department.

Sheila Gionfriddo, Science Discipline

Sheila is currently a faculty member at Luzerne County Community College, teaching various computer application courses, office information courses, health information management, and ICD-10 and CPT coding courses. She has been an educator for 16 years at the college, starting as an adjunct and then as a full-time faculty member. She is the coordinator for the Office Information Management program and Administrator for MyITLab at the college. She is Microsoft certified in all Office Applications. Sheila received a B.S. from the University of Connecticut, an A.A.S. degree in Computer Information Systems from Luzerne County Community College, and is a certified medical coder. After working almost twenty years for the American Red Cross, she switched careers. With a strong science background and a love of learning, she pursued degrees in computer and health information technologies. One of her greatest joys is helping students of all ages and backgrounds to learn how to use computer applications and programs to be successful in their chosen field of study.

Lynn Hogan, Education Discipline

Lynn Hogan teaches at the University of North Alabama, providing instruction in the area of computer applications. With more than 30 years of educational experience at the community college and university level, Lynn has taught applications, programming, and concepts courses in both online and classroom environments. She received an M.B.A. from the University of North Alabama and a Ph.D. from the University of Alabama.

Rebecca Lawson, Business Discipline

Rebecca Lawson is a professor in the Computer Information Technologies program at Lansing Community College. She coordinates the curriculum, develops the instructional materials, and teaches for the E-Business curriculum. She also serves as the Online Faculty Coordinator at the Center for Teaching Excellence at LCC. In that role, she develops and facilitates online workshops for faculty learning to teach online. Her major areas of interest include online curriculum quality assurance, the review and development of printed and online instructional materials, the assessment of computer and Internet literary skill levels to facilitate student retention, and the use of social networking tools to support learning in blended and online learning environments.

Dr. Anthony Nowakowski, Arts Discipline

Dr. Anthony Nowakowski has taught mathematics and computer-related courses spanning more than fifty years to students ranging from 7th grade to graduate-school level. He is a Professor Emeritus in the Computer Information Systems department at Buffalo State College. Although retired, he continues to teach Visual Basic programming courses both face-to-face and online. Anthony holds a Ph.D. degree in Mathematics Education from the State University of New York at Buffalo, an M.A. degree in Mathematics, and a B.S. degree in Secondary Mathematics Education, both from the State University College at Buffalo.

Contents

Acknowledgments

The Exploring team acknowledges and thanks all the reviewers who helped us throughout the years by providing us with their invaluable comments, suggestions, and constructive criticism.

Adriana Lumpkin
Midland College

Alan S. Abrahams
Virginia Tech

Alexandre C. Probst
Colorado Christian University

Ali Berrached
University of Houston–Downtown

Allen Alexander
Delaware Technical & Community College

Andrea Marchese
Maritime College, State University of New York

Andrew Blitz
Broward College; Edison State College

Angel Norman
University of Tennessee, Knoxville

Angela Clark
University of South Alabama

Ann Rovetto
Horry-Georgetown Technical College

Astrid Todd
Guilford Technical Community College

Audrey Gillant
Maritime College, State University of New York

Barbara Stover
Marion Technical College

Barbara Tollinger
Sinclair Community College

Ben Brahim Taha
Auburn University

Beverly Amer
Northern Arizona University

Beverly Fite
Amarillo College

Biswadip Ghosh
Metropolitan State University of Denver

Bonita Volker
Tidewater Community College

Bonnie Homan
San Francisco State University

Brad West
Sinclair Community College

Brian Powell
West Virginia University

Carol Buser
Owens Community College

Carol Roberts
University of Maine

Carolyn Barren
Macomb Community College

Carolyn Borne
Louisiana State University

Cathy Poyner
Truman State University

Charles Hodgson
Delgado Community College

Chen Zhang
Bryant University

Cheri Higgins
Illinois State University

Cheryl Brown
Delgado Community College

Cheryl Hinds
Norfolk State University

Cheryl Sypniewski
Macomb Community College

Chris Robinson
Northwest State Community College

Cindy Herbert
Metropolitan Community College–Longview

Craig J. Peterson
American InterContinental University

Dana Hooper
University of Alabama

Dana Johnson
North Dakota State University

Daniela Marghitu
Auburn University

David Noel
University of Central Oklahoma

David Pulis
Maritime College, State University of New York

David Thornton
Jacksonville State University

Dawn Medlin
Appalachian State University

Debby Keen
University of Kentucky

Debra Chapman
University of South Alabama

Debra Hoffman
Southeast Missouri State University

Derrick Huang
Florida Atlantic University

Diana Baran
Henry Ford Community College

Diane Cassidy
The University of North Carolina at Charlotte

Diane L. Smith
Henry Ford Community College

Dick Hewer
Ferris State College

Don Danner
San Francisco State University

Don Hoggan
Solano College

Don Riggs
SUNY Schenectady County Community College

Doncho Petkov
Eastern Connecticut State University

Donna Ehrhart
State University of New York at Brockport

Elaine Crable
Xavier University

Elizabeth Duett
Delgado Community College

Erhan Uskup
Houston Community College–Northwest

Eric Martin
University of Tennessee

Erika Nadas
Wilbur Wright College

Floyd Winters
Manatee Community College

Frank Lucente
Westmoreland County Community College

G. Jan Wilms
Union University

Gail Cope
Sinclair Community College

Gary DeLorenzo
California University of Pennsylvania

Gary Garrison
Belmont University

Gary McFall
Purdue University

George Cassidy
Sussex County Community College

Gerald Braun
Xavier University

Gerald Burgess
Western New Mexico University

Gladys Swindler
Fort Hays State University

Hector Frausto
California State University Los Angeles

Heith Hennel
Valencia Community College

Henry Rudzinski
Central Connecticut State University

Irene Joos
La Roche College

Iwona Rusin
Baker College; Davenport University

J. Roberto Guzman
San Diego Mesa College

Jacqueline D. Lawson
Henry Ford Community College

Jakie Brown Jr.
Stevenson University

James Brown
Central Washington University

James Powers
University of Southern Indiana

Jane Stam
Onondaga Community College

Janet Bringhurst
Utah State University

Jean Welsh
Lansing Community College

Jeanette Dix
Ivy Tech Community College

Jennifer Day
Sinclair Community College

Jill Canine
Ivy Tech Community College

Jill Young
Southeast Missouri State University

Jim Chaffee
The University of Iowa Tippie College of Business

Joanne Lazirko
University of Wisconsin–Milwaukee

Jodi Milliner
Kansas State University

John Hollenbeck
Blue Ridge Community College

John Seydel
Arkansas State University

Judith A. Scheeren
Westmoreland County Community College

Judith Brown
The University of Memphis

Juliana Cypert
Tarrant County College

Kamaljeet Sanghera
George Mason University

Karen Priestly
Northern Virginia Community College

Karen Ravan
Spartanburg Community College

Karen Tracey
Central Connecticut State University

Kathleen Brenan
Ashland University

Ken Busbee
Houston Community College

Kent Foster
Winthrop University

Kevin Anderson
Solano Community College

Kim Wright
The University of Alabama

Kristen Hockman
University of Missouri–Columbia

Kristi Smith
Allegany College of Maryland

Laura Marcoulides
Fullerton College

Laura McManamon
University of Dayton

Laurence Boxer
Niagara University

Leanne Chun
Leeward Community College

Lee McClain
Western Washington University

Linda D. Collins
Mesa Community College

Linda Johnsonius
Murray State University

Linda Lau
Longwood University

Linda Theus
Jackson State Community College

Linda Williams
Marion Technical College

Lisa Miller
University of Central Oklahoma

Lister Horn
Pensacola Junior College

Lixin Tao
Pace University

Loraine Miller
Cayuga Community College

Lori Kielty
Central Florida Community College

Lorna Wells
Salt Lake Community College

Lorraine Sauchin
Duquesne University

Lucy Parakhovnik
California State University, Northridge

Lynn Keane
University of South Carolina

Lynn Mancini
Delaware Technical Community College

Mackinzee Escamilla
South Plains College

Marcia Welch
Highline Community College

Margaret McManus
Northwest Florida State College

Margaret Warrick
Allan Hancock College

Marilyn Hibbert
Salt Lake Community College

Mark Choman
Luzerne County Community College

Maryann Clark
University of New Hampshire

Mary Beth Tarver
Northwestern State University

Mary Duncan
University of Missouri–St. Louis

Melissa Nemeth
Indiana University-Purdue University Indianapolis

Melody Alexander
Ball State University

Michael Douglas
University of Arkansas at Little Rock

Michael Dunklebarger
Alamance Community College

Michael G. Skaff
College of the Sequoias

Michele Budnovitch
Pennsylvania College of Technology

Mike Jochen
East Stroudsburg University

Mike Michaelson
Palomar College

Mike Scroggins
Missouri State University

Mimi Spain
Southern Maine Community College

Muhammed Badamas
Morgan State University

NaLisa Brown
University of the Ozarks

Nancy Grant
Community College of Allegheny County–South Campus

Nanette Lareau
University of Arkansas Community College–Morrilton

Nikia Robinson
Indian River State University

Pam Brune
Chattanooga State Community College

Pam Uhlenkamp
Iowa Central Community College

Patrick Smith
Marshall Community and Technical College

Paul Addison
Ivy Tech Community College

Paula Ruby
Arkansas State University

Peggy Burrus
Red Rocks Community College

Peter Ross
SUNY Albany

Philip H. Nielson
Salt Lake Community College

Philip Valvalides
Guilford Technical Community College

Ralph Hooper
University of Alabama

Ranette Halverson
Midwestern State University

Richard Blamer
John Carroll University

Richard Cacace
Pensacola Junior College

Richard Hewer
Ferris State University

Richard Sellers
Hill College

Rob Murray
Ivy Tech Community College

Robert Banta
Macomb Community College

Robert Dušek
Northern Virginia Community College

Robert G. Phipps Jr.
West Virginia University

Robert Sindt
Johnson County Community College

Robert Warren
Delgado Community College

Rocky Belcher
Sinclair Community College

Roger Pick
University of Missouri at Kansas City

Ronnie Creel
Troy University

Rosalie Westerberg
Clover Park Technical College

Ruth Neal
Navarro College

Sandra Thomas
Troy University

Sheila Gionfriddo
Luzerne County Community College

Sherrie Geitgey
Northwest State Community College

Sherry Lenhart
Terra Community College

Sophia Wilberscheid
Indian River State College

Sophie Lee
California State University, Long Beach

Stacy Johnson
Iowa Central Community College

Stephanie Kramer
Northwest State Community College

Stephen Z. Jourdan
Auburn University at Montgomery

Steven Schwarz
Raritan Valley Community College

Sue A. McCrory
Missouri State University

Sumathy Chandrashekar
Salisbury University

Susan Fuschetto
Cerritos College

Susan Medlin
UNC Charlotte

Susan N. Dozier
Tidewater Community College

Suzan Spitzberg
Oakton Community College

Suzanne M. Jeska
County College of Morris

Sven Aelterman
Troy University

Sy Hirsch
Sacred Heart University

Sylvia Brown
Midland College

Tanya Patrick
Clackamas Community College

Terri Holly
Indian River State College

Terry Ray Rigsby
Hill College

Thomas Rienzo
Western Michigan University

Tina Johnson
Midwestern State University

Tommy Lu
Delaware Technical Community College

Troy S. Cash
Northwest Arkansas Community College

Vicki Robertson
Southwest Tennessee Community

Vickie Pickett
Midland College

Weifeng Chen
California University of Pennsylvania

Wes Anthony
Houston Community College

William Ayen
University of Colorado at Colorado Springs

Wilma Andrews
Virginia Commonwealth University

Yvonne Galusha
University of Iowa

Special thanks to our content development and technical team:

Barbara Stover
Patti Hammerle
Morgan Hetzler
Joyce Nielsen

Preface

The Exploring Series and You

Exploring is Pearson's Office Application series that requires students like you to think "beyond the point and click." In this edition, we have worked to restructure the Exploring experience around the way you, today's modern student, actually use your resources.

The goal of Exploring is, as it has always been, to go farther than teaching just the steps to accomplish a task—the series provides the theoretical foundation for you to understand when and why to apply a skill. As a result, you achieve a deeper understanding of each application and can apply this critical thinking beyond Office and the classroom.

The How & Why of This Revision

Outcomes matter. Whether it's getting a good grade in this course, learning how to use Microsoft Office and Windows 10 so students can be successful in other courses, or learning a specific skill that will make learners successful in a future job, everyone has an outcome in mind. And outcomes matter. That is why we revised our chapter opener to focus on the outcomes students will achieve by working through each Exploring chapter. These are coupled with objectives and skills, providing a map students can follow to get everything they need from each chapter.

Critical Thinking and Collaboration are essential 21st-century skills. Students want and need to be successful in their future careers—so we used motivating case studies to show relevance of these skills to future careers.

Students today read, prepare, and study differently than students used to. Students use textbooks like a tool—they want to easily identify what they need to know and learn it efficiently. We have added key features, such as Tasks Lists (in purple) and Step Icons, and tracked everything via page numbers that allow efficient navigation, creating a map students can easily follow.

Students are exposed to technology. The new edition of Exploring moves beyond the basics of the software at a faster pace, without sacrificing coverage of the fundamental skills that students need to know.

Students are diverse. Students can be any age, any gender, any race, with any level of ability or learning style. With this in mind, we broadened our definition of "student resources" to include MyITLab, the most powerful and most ADA-compliant online homework and assessment tool around with a direct 1:1 content match with the Exploring Series. Exploring will be accessible to all students, regardless of learning style.

Providing You with a Map to Success to Move Beyond the Point and Click

All of these changes and additions will provide students an easy and efficient path to follow to be successful in this course, regardless of where they start at the beginning of this course. Our goal is to keep students engaged in both the hands-on and conceptual sides, helping achieve a higher level of understanding that will guarantee success in this course and in a future career.

In addition to the vision and experience of the series creator, Robert T. Grauer, we have assembled a tremendously talented team of Office Applications authors who have devoted themselves to teaching the ins and outs of Microsoft Word, Excel, Access, and PowerPoint. Led in this edition by series editor Mary Anne Poatsy, the whole team is dedicated to the Exploring mission of moving students **beyond the point and click**.

Resources

Instructor Resources

The Instructor's Resource Center, available at **www.pearsonhighered.com**, includes the following:

- **Instructor Manual** provides one-stop-shop for instructors, including an overview of all available resources, teaching tips, as well as student data and solution files for every exercise.
- **Solution Files with Scorecards** assist with grading the Hands-On Exercises and end-of-chapter exercises.

Student Resources

Student Data Files

Access your student data files needed to complete the exercises in this textbook at **www.pearsonhighered.com/exploring.**

Available in MyITLab

- **eText** available in some MyITLab courses and includes links to videos, student data files, and other learning aids.

Arts Discipline

DISCIPLINE 1

Using Office in the Arts

Jacob Lund/Fotolia

LEARNING OUTCOMES

- **You will use Word to create a formatted Word document, with tables, media, and imported text, which you can share with others.**
- **You will use Excel to create a multi-worksheet workbook that uses functions and formulas, to perform a variety of calculations, and pie charts to help visualize the data.**
- **You will use Access to create and modify database objects—tables, queries, forms, and reports—sort and filter the data, use functions and calculations to display results, and apply formatting.**
- **You will use PowerPoint to create dynamic multimedia presentations for delivery to an audience and to display in a kiosk.**
- **You will use a combination of the individual strengths of the Office 2016 applications using Excel's calculating and charting features, Access' data management capabilities, and PowerPoint's presentation ability by importing and linking information among them.**

CASE STUDY | Working as a Production Assistant

Production work in theater, film-making, and television requires the assistance of many workers. The production assistant, also called a *PA,* may have a vast number of responsibilities that can be as rudimentary as going for a cup of coffee to being in an administrative level of managing actors and staff, and then handling many aspects of public relations.

Microsoft Office provides a suite of applications to assist a theater company PA with many administrative tasks, including creating a press packet for the company. Such a packet would include a cover page, a cover letter, a press release, and a brochure to advertise upcoming productions. The PA may be responsible for overseeing the finances of a production by maintaining schedules, analyzing the budget for upcoming shows, updating the budget of a current show, and forecasting ticket sales based on past shows. Much of the data can be stored in databases to give the PA immediate access to generating forms and reports that will be used by producers and directors. A kiosk is located in the theater, and the PA will be responsible for creating and maintaining presentation files that can run automatically and advertise season tickets for the year.

Production Assistants

Use Microsoft Word

Background

A word-processing application is the most used program in a theater-company business office. Production assistants create correspondence, contracts with actors, and theater rental space contracts as well as memos, reports, press releases, and documents requiring desktop publishing. It is imperative that a production assistant becomes proficient in Microsoft Word and its many features.

Skills:

Chapter 1

Apply Font Attributes, Check Spelling and Grammar, Insert Headers and Footers, Set Margins

Chapter 2

Apply Borders; Apply Styles; Insert a Text Box; Insert and Modify WordArt; Insert Page Breaks; Insert, Resize, Move, and Align a Picture; Select a Document Theme; Select Paragraph Spacing; Set off Paragraphs with Tabs and Bulleted Lists; Use Styles

Chapter 3

Convert Text to a Table, Format a Table, Insert a Row or Column, Insert a Table, Insert Formulas in a Table, Merge Cells

Chapter 4

Accept Changes, Add a Comment, Create Footnotes, Insert a Cover Page, Use Track Changes

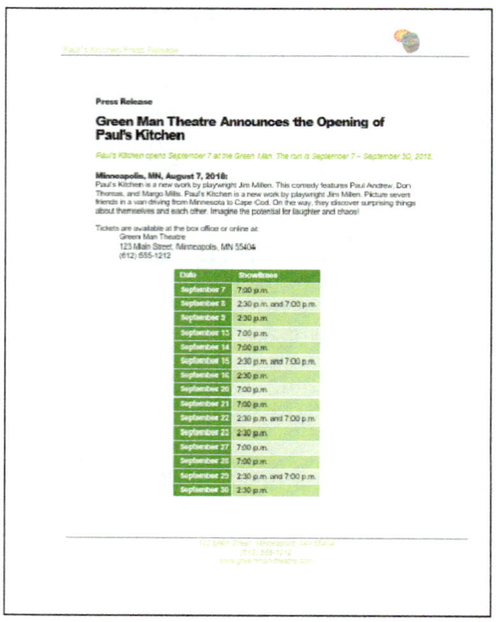

Paul's Kitchen Press Release

Press Release

Green Man Theatre Announces the Opening of Paul's Kitchen

Paul's Kitchen opens September 7 at the Green Man. The run is September 7 – September 30, 2018.

Minneapolis, MN, August 7, 2018:
Paul's Kitchen is a new work by playwright Jim Millen. This comedy features Paul Andrew, Don Thomas, and Margo Mills. Paul's Kitchen is a new work by playwright Jim Millen. Picture seven friends in a van driving from Minnesota to Cape Cod. On the way, they discover surprising things about themselves and each other. Imagine the potential for laughter and chaos!

Tickets are available at the box office or online at:
Green Man Theatre
123 Main Street, Minneapolis, MN 55404
(612) 555-1212

Date	Showtimes
September 7	7:00 p.m.
September 8	2:30 p.m. and 7:00 p.m.
September 9	2:30 p.m.
September 13	7:00 p.m.
September 14	7:00 p.m.
September 15	2:30 p.m. and 7:00 p.m.
September 16	2:30 p.m.
September 20	7:00 p.m.
September 21	7:00 p.m.
September 22	2:30 p.m. and 7:00 p.m.
September 23	2:30 p.m.
September 27	7:00 p.m.
September 28	7:00 p.m.
September 29	2:30 p.m. and 7:00 p.m.
September 30	2:30 p.m.

Word 2016, Windows 10, Microsoft Corporation

FIGURE 1.1 Production Assistant Documents

CASE STUDY | Working as a Production Assistant

Starting Files	Files to be Submitted
01w_PressPacket **01w_gmlogo.jpg** **01w_PriceList**	**01w_PressPacket_LastFirst**

Capstone Exercises

You work as a production assistant in the offices of a new company, the Green Man Theatre. You have been asked to create a press packet for Paul's Kitchen, *a Green Man production. The packet will include a cover page, a cover letter, a press release, and a brochure advertising upcoming Green Man productions.*

Create a Cover Page

You create a cover page for the press packet that introduces the *Paul's Kitchen* production and includes the date of the packet release and your name as the contact person for further information. You include the Green Man logo on the cover page and all other materials in the press packet for quick visual recognition.

a. Open *01w_PressPacket*, and save it as **01w_PressPacket_LastFirst**.

b. Turn on **Show/Hide** to help you work with the multiple sections you will be creating for the press packet.

c. Set the document margins to **Normal**.

d. Insert a cover page in the **Semaphore** style. Change the document theme to **Facet**.

e. Type **Paul's Kitchen Press Release** as the document title. Type **Presented by Green Man Theater** as the document subtitle. Note: When used in a proper name, it is spelled *theatre*. This error will be corrected later.

f. Enter today's date using the Date Control. Remove the text boxes that contain the Author, Company name, and Address content controls.

g. Press **Ctrl+Home** to move the insertion point to the first paragraph mark at the top of the page. Press **Enter** twice and insert a **Sideline Quote text box**. Type the following contact information using your email address for the requested email address:

   Your Name

   Production Assistant

   Green Man Theatre

   Phone: 1 (612) 555–1212

   Fax: 1 (612) 444–2323

   Email:

h. Place the insertion point at the paragraph mark below the date. Insert the *01w_gmlogo* file and apply the **Square text wrapping style**. Apply **Align Middle** and **Align Center** to move the logo image down on the page.

i. Create a WordArt object on the cover page using the WordArt style **Fill: Dark Green, Accent color 2, Outline: Dark Green, Accent color 2** and **Green Man Theatre** as the text. Change the Font to **Times New Roman**, change the Text Fill color to **Green, Accent 1, Darker 25%**, change the Text Outline color to **Red**, and then select the Outer Shadow style named **Offset: Top Left**. Apply the **Square text wrapping style** and move the WordArt to appear above the logo with text not overlapping the image. Apply **Align Center** to the WordArt.

Create a Cover Letter

You write a cover letter to members of the press inviting them to the *Paul's Kitchen* production and offering them four complimentary tickets.

a. Place the insertion point at the beginning of the first line of the second page and insert a page break to add a blank page between the cover and press release pages. You will create a cover letter on this blank page.

b. Place the insertion point on the blank page before the page break, press Enter, and move to the blank line.

c. Type a return address block using the following information:

   Green Man Theatre

   123 Main Street

   Minneapolis, MN 55404

d. Insert three blank lines after the return address and add a date that will automatically update. Use the Month Day, Year format.

e. Press **Enter** four times, type **Greetings Members of the Press:** as a salutation line, and then press **Enter** two times.

f. Type the following text for the cover letter, making sure there is **6 pt** spacing before and after each paragraph you create:

   Green Man Theatre's 2018 season is opening with a production of *Paul's Kitchen*, the story of seven friends, one van, and lots of laughs.

   The press will find the following information in the press packet:

   - Press release
   - Ticket price list
   - Brochure

   The press member is personally invited to enjoy a performance of *Paul's Kitchen*. The press member needs to present the press packet at the box office to receive their four complimentary tickets.

g. Insert a complimentary closing line followed by a comma.

h. Leave three blank lines after the complimentary closing line, type your name, and then press **Enter**.

i. Type **Production Assistant** as your title on the next line following your name.

j. Insert the **Grid header** to the cover letter. (*Note:* If the header text is not capitalized correctly, correct the title content control on the cover page.) Delete the Date Control in the header. Add a **Bottom Border** to the header. Copy the logo from the cover page and paste it into the header. Resize the logo and use an appropriate wrapping style so that it fits attractively above the border line.

k. Add a **Semaphore footer**. Replace the page number text with the theater's contact information, displayed in three lines with no space before paragraphs:

   123 Main Street, Minneapolis, MN 55404

   (612) 555-1212

   www.greenman-theatre.com

l. Set the Footer from Bottom distance to **0.5"** in each section. Add a **Top Border** to the footer. Close the header and footer.

m. Use Page Setup to change the page layout so that its vertical alignment is set to **center**.

Modify the Press Release

The basic information for the press release is on page 3 of the packet, but needs to be formatted professionally. You format the press release.

a. Apply the **Emphasis style** to the text *Press Release* on page 3 of the press packet.

b. Change the style of the text *Green Man Theatre Announces the Opening of Paul's Kitchen* to the **Title style**.

c. Apply the **Intense Emphasis style** to the paragraph that begins *Paul's Kitchen opens.*

d. Change the style of the line that begins *Minneapolis* to the **Emphasis style**.

e. Move the insertion point to the second blank line following the paragraph that introduces the playwright and actors, and describes the basic plot of the play. Type **Tickets are available at the box office or online at:** and press **Enter**.

f. Press **Tab** and type the following address information on the next three lines, adding a tab at the beginning of the second and third lines:

Green Man Theatre

123 Main Street, Minneapolis, MN 55404

(612) 555–1212

Convert the Showtimes Table

To make the showtimes of *Paul's Kitchen* easier to read, you apply a table format that matches the theme you used on the cover page.

a. Convert the text listing dates and showtimes to a two-column table.

b. Format the table using the **Grid Table 5 Dark – Accent 2 table style**.

c. Adjust the width of the first column so that the month and the day are not split.

d. Change the row height to **0.25"**.

e. Align the text in the table cells so that the text is centered vertically and aligned to the left side of the cells.

f. AutoFit the table contents.

g. Center the table horizontally on the page.

Create a New Ticket Price List

You add a table to the press packet that displays the ticket types available and the costs per type of ticket. You format the table to match the theme colors.

a. Insert a **Page Break** after the table for a blank page.

b. Create a table with four columns and four rows.

c. Format the table using the **Grid Table 5 Dark – Accent 2 table style**.

d. Merge the cells of the top row, type the title **Green Man Theatre Ticket Price List** in the merged cell, apply the **Title style** to the title, and then center the title.

e. Type the following headings, beginning in the second row and first column:

Ticket Type	At the Door	Advance Purchase	Season Tickets
Adult			
Senior			

f. Insert a row above the *Adult* row and type **Student** as the *Ticket Type*.

g. Enter the *At the Door* ticket prices as shown:

Student	**$15**
Adult	**$50**
Senior	**$25**

h. Enter formulas with $ number format in the table to calculate the ticket prices using these discounts:
   - A 20% discount for all advance purchase tickets.
   - A 25% discount for season tickets. The season ticket price is the equivalent of purchasing tickets to all three productions.

i. Apply the **Normal Style** to all rows of text and change the font size to **14 pt**.

j. Set the table preferred width to **6.65"**.

k. Add a footnote to the Advance Purchase column heading: **Advance Purchase tickets receive a 20% discount and must be purchased at least two weeks before the show.**

l. Add a footnote to the Season Tickets column heading: **Season tickets receive a 25% discount. All three tickets of the season must be purchased at once to qualify for season ticket pricing.**

m. Press **Enter** twice for spacing between the footnotes and footer section. Place the insertion point below the ticket price table and press **Enter**.

Insert a Merchandise Price List

The Theatre Shop manager asked you to include a price list of merchandise in the press packet. You will copy and paste the table from the file containing these prices.

a. Open the file *01w_PriceList*, copy the price list table, and close the file. Paste the table beneath the *Green Man Theatre Ticket Price List*.

b. Format the table using the **List Table 4 – Accent 2 table style**.

c. Apply the **Title style** to the table title and center the title. Change the font size to **10 pt** in the rows below the title.

d. Apply Align Center Left to the Item column and apply Align Center to the Price and Patron Discount columns.

e. Change the Green Man Theatre Mug price to $8.00. Position the insertion point to the right of the mug price, and press F9 to update the fields.

Complete a Document Review

You proofread the press packet and note that some of the references to Green Man Theatre use *Theater* in the name instead of *Theatre*. After proofreading, you review the document by checking the spelling and grammar of each page. Finally, before presenting the press packet to the Board of Directors for approval, you add a question to the Board.

a. Turn on **Track Changes**.

b. Use Smart Lookup to find the definition of *Theater*. Find all occurrences of *Theater* within *Green Man Theater* and replace with **Theatre** so that the company name is *Green Man Theatre*.

c. Check the spelling and grammar of the packet. Accept all references to *showtimes* as the correct spelling.

d. Accept all remaining changes and stop tracking.
e. Select the phrase *four complimentary tickets* in the cover letter and add a comment: **Did we decide on two tickets or four tickets?**
f. Save and close the file. Based on your instructor's directions, submit 01w_PressPacket_LastFirst.

Production Assistants

Use Microsoft Excel

Background

Green Man Theatre is a local production company that puts on productions of plays and musicals. It has a small staff that takes care of production details, such as finances, scheduling, auditions, and so on. Community actors audition for roles in plays and are paid a small stipend. A production assistant uses spreadsheets to prepare budgets for current and upcoming plays and musicals, as well as prepare rehearsal schedules for current shows and financial reports based on past shows. Therefore, it is imperative that theater production assistants are proficient in using Microsoft Excel.

Skills:

Chapter 1

Apply a Cell Style, Apply Alignment and Font Options, Apply Number Formats, Apply the Order of Operations, Apply Wrap Text, Copy Formulas with Auto Fill, Create Headers and Footers, Increase and Decrease Decimal Places, Increase Indent, Insert Basic Statistical Functions, Insert Rows, Manage Worksheets, Merge and Center Data, Set Page Orientation, Enter and Edit Cell Data, Use Cell References in Formulas

Chapter 2

Calculate a Total with the SUM Function, Insert the TODAY Function, Use LOOKUP Function, Use the IF Function, Use the PMT Function

Chapter 3

Apply a Chart Style, Choose a Chart Type, Create a Pie Chart, Move a Chart, Select Data Source for a Chart

Chapter 4

Apply a Table Style, Apply Conditional Formatting, Apply Text Filters, Create a Custom Sort, Create a Table, Sort Multiple Fields

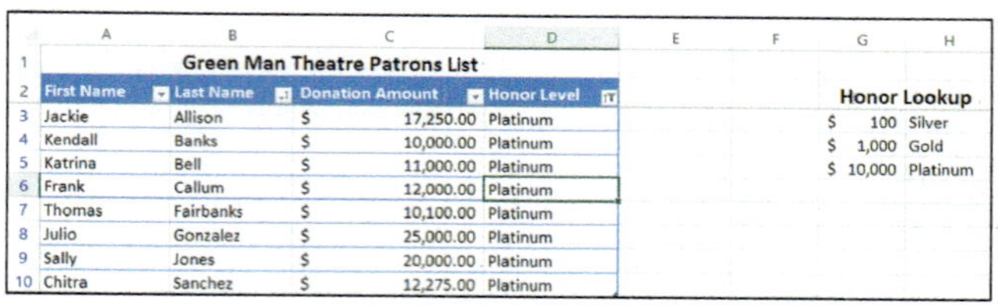

	A	B	C	D	E	F	G	H
1	Green Man Theatre Patrons List							
2	First Name	Last Name	Donation Amount	Honor Level			Honor Lookup	
3	Jackie	Allison	$ 17,250.00	Platinum			$ 100	Silver
4	Kendall	Banks	$ 10,000.00	Platinum			$ 1,000	Gold
5	Katrina	Bell	$ 11,000.00	Platinum			$ 10,000	Platinum
6	Frank	Callum	$ 12,000.00	Platinum				
7	Thomas	Fairbanks	$ 10,100.00	Platinum				
8	Julio	Gonzalez	$ 25,000.00	Platinum				
9	Sally	Jones	$ 20,000.00	Platinum				
10	Chitra	Sanchez	$ 12,275.00	Platinum				

FIGURE 1.2 Production Assistant Workbook

CASE STUDY | Working as a Production Assistant

Starting File	File to be Submitted
01e_Theatre	01e_Theatre_LastFirst

Capstone Exercises

You work as a production assistant for the Green Man Theatre. The director of operations asked you to prepare a packet to include an audition schedule and a budget for the upcoming show, Paul's Kitchen. *In addition, she asked you to update the budget for the current show and create a chart. Finally, you need to create a forecast of ticket sales based on past shows. Rehearsals run for four weeks, starting Monday, August 6, 2018. The show opens Friday, September 7, 2018, just after the Labor Day weekend.*

Complete a Proposed Budget for *Paul's Kitchen*

You need to compile data to create a proposed budget for *Paul's Kitchen*, the first show of the Green Man Theatre's 2018 season. The workbook contains some of the weekly salary and expense data you have already received from the director, stage manager, prop master, costume designer, and tech crew. You will enter and format some data and calculate total weekly expenses and categorical totals for the two-month period.

a. Open *01e_Theatre* and save it as **01e_Theatre_LastFirst**.

b. Rename *Sheet1* as **Budget Kitchen**. This sheet contains the proposed budget for the production of *Paul's Kitchen*.

c. Enter a function in **cell A2** that displays the current date each time you open the workbook.

d. Format the title *Budget for Paul's Kitchen* so that it is centered across columns A:K. Apply the **Accent1 cell style**, **16 pt font**, and adjust the row height to **23**. Align the text so that it is aligned between the top and bottom of the cell.

e. Format the **range A3:K18** using **Calibri 12 pt**. Center and bold the column labels in **cells B3:K3**. Widen the columns to ensure all data is displayed.

f. Insert a row above **cell A4** and enter the text **Salaries** in **cell A4**. Indent the row labels in **cells A5:A15** to categorize these rows as salaried positions.

g. Insert a row above **cell A16**, and enter the text **Other Expenses** in **cell A16** at the left margin and not indented as the cells above. Indent the row labels in **cells A17:A19** to categorize these rows as other expenses.

h. Enter data for salaries in **cells B6:J7**. The actors' salaries are 1500 per week, and the stage manager earns 200 per week.

i. Format the **range B5:K20** with **Accounting Number Format** and with no decimal places.

j. Insert a formula in **cell K5** to calculate the total nine-week salary for the director. Use the fill handle to copy the formula to **cell K19** and delete the contents of **cell K16**.

k. Calculate the weekly total expenses in **cell B20**. Copy the formula for the rest of the totals on row 20.

l. Apply the **Total cell style** to the **range A20:K20** and adjust the column width of column K if necessary to ensure all data is displayed.

m. Save the workbook.

Calculate Projected Revenue and Net Profit

The bottom section of the Budget Kitchen worksheet contains Projected Ticket Sales. This section contains ticket prices by group and projected number of advance and door ticket sales. Green Man Theatre gives a 25% discount for tickets purchased in advance. You need to insert cells to make room for the advanced sales price per group and calculate the projected revenue.

a. Merge and center the title across the **range A23:F23**. Use Format Painter to copy formatting from **cell A1** to **cell A23**.
b. Type **Advance Discount** in **cell G24** Type **.25** in **cell G25**. Apply **Percent Style** with no decimal places.
c. Insert cells in the **range C24:C27** by shifting the existing cells to the right. Type **Advance Sales** in **cell C24**.
d. Format the labels in the **range B24:H24** with wrap text, bold, and centering.
e. Use the data in cells **B25** and **H25** and create a formula that calculates the advance sales price for the Senior Citizens group. The formula should subtract the discount rate from 1 and multiply that difference by the contents of **cell B25**. Use relative and absolute cell references appropriately. Copy this formula to Adults and Students.
f. Enter a formula in **cell F25** that calculates total ticket revenue for projected senior citizen ticket sales. Copy the formula for the other two groups.
g. Calculate the total projected number of advance and door tickets sold in **cells D28** and **E28**, respectively. Calculate the total projected ticket sale revenue in **cell F28** and format with **Accounting Number Format and with no decimal places**.
h. Apply a **Total cell style** to the **range A28:F28**.
i. Merge and center the **range A30:B30**. Use Format Painter to copy the formats from **cell A23** to **cell A30**.
j. Enter a formula in **cell B31** that displays the total projected ticket sales revenue that is stored in cell F28.
k. Enter a formula in **cell B32** that displays the total expenses that is stored in cell K20.
l. Enter a formula in **cell B33** that calculates the total profit after expenses.
m. Check for column widths and consistent no-decimal formats. Revise cell formats as needed.
n. Apply **landscape orientation**. Create a footer that displays your name on the left side, the sheet tab code in the center, and the file name code on the right side.
o. Save the workbook.

Use the IF Function

Because actors work as independent contractors, they are reimbursed for mileage. The Green Man Theatre has an optional equal mileage payment plan that cast members can opt into to reduce the amount of paperwork. You have collected each of their round trip distances to the theater and have created an equalized mileage reimbursement based on whether they participate in the Mileage Payment Plan or not. The actors opting out of the equal mileage payment plan will turn in expense reports including their mileage logs and will receive mileage reimbursement in a lump sum at the end of the production based on their mileage logs.

a. Display the Mileage sheet.
b. Create a formula in **cell B7** to calculate miles driven by Ellen Anderson for all rehearsals and performances. The total number of rehearsals and performances is stored in **cell B12**. Use relative and absolute cell references appropriately. Copy the formula for the rest of the cast.
c. Create a formula in **cell B8** to calculate the total mileage reimbursement for Ellen Anderson. The reimbursement rate is stored in **cell B11**. Use relative and absolute cell references appropriately. Copy the formula for the rest of the cast.

d. Create an IF function in **cell B9** that equally divides the total mileage payments across the weekly pay periods for the production cycle of the show if the cast member opts into the Mileage Equal Payment Plan as indicated in row 5. If the cast member does not participate in the Mileage Equal Payment Plan, the function returns 0. The number of weeks of the production cycle is in **cell B13**. Use relative and absolute cell references appropriately. Copy this function for the rest of the cast.

e. Save the workbook.

Prepare Mileage Statistics

To help prepare budgets accurately for future productions, you prepare statistics on mileage expense reimbursement for each production. Because the number of actors varies from production to production, you need statistics on mileage reimbursement for a single actor.

a. Enter a function in **cell B16** to calculate the minimum total mileage reimbursement.

b. Enter a function in **cell B17** to calculate the maximum total mileage reimbursement.

c. Enter a function in **cell B18** to calculate the average total mileage reimbursement.

d. Enter a function in **cell B19** to calculate the total mileage reimbursement.

e. Apply **landscape orientation.**

f. Save the workbook.

Calculate a Loan Payment

Part of your responsibility in managing the budget is to make recommendations on loan expenses. The Board of Directors has voted to replace the sound system and take out a loan to finance the cost. A theater patron is the president of a local bank. She has guaranteed an interest rate of 4.25% on a five-year loan for the sound system. The board approved the purchase of an $18,995 sound system, including installation. How much will the monthly payment be on the loan?

a. Display the Sound System worksheet.

b. Enter the input values in **column B**, as mentioned in the above paragraph. Green Man Theatre will make monthly payments, so type **12** for the number of payments in one year.

c. Insert a **PMT function** in **cell B6** to calculate the monthly payment. Be sure the result displays as a positive number.

d. Save the workbook.

Use a Lookup Function

The Green Man Theatre has created an Honor Circle to thank their most generous patrons. The required donations for each level in the Honor Circle are listed in the following table. One of your responsibilities is to keep track of patrons' donations and give them appropriate acknowledgments in the playbill. You will use a lookup function to assign the appropriate Honor Level to your Patrons list. You will then apply conditional formatting to the table to highlight Silver members to be targeted for additional donations next year. To ensure Platinum members are recognized on the program, you will filter the list.

Silver	$100
Gold	$1,000
Platinum	$10,000

a. Display the Patrons worksheet.
b. Create a lookup table starting in **cell G3** using the above table. Make sure the data is organized appropriately for a lookup table.
c. Apply **Accounting Number Format** with no decimal places to the values and **General format** for the text. Assign a range name **Honor_Lookup** to the lookup table.
d. Using **Honor_Lookup**, create a **VLOOKUP function** in **cell D3** that returns the honor level based on each patron's gift.
e. Copy this function for the rest of the patrons.
f. Select the **range A2:D43** and convert it to a table. Apply the **Table Style Light 9 style**.
g. Freeze the header row so the column headings will always be visible.
h. Create a custom sort list to sort the table by Honor Level so Platinum patrons are at the top of the list, then Gold, and finally Silver. Sort the patrons alphabetically by last name inside the Honor Level groupings.
i. Apply conditional formatting to the table to highlight members that donated between $700 and $1,000 using **Green Fill with Dark Green Text** as the highlighting color.
j. Copy the Patrons sheet and name it Platinum. Filter the Patrons table to display only the Platinum members.
k. Save the workbook.

Create a Budget Summary

After a successful run of *Paul's Kitchen*, you create a budget summary and charts summarizing ticket sales. Remarkably enough, the production stayed on budget and Green Man Theatre's ticket sales projections were pretty accurate.

a. Copy the Budget Kitchen worksheet and rename the copied sheet **Budget Summary**. Move the Budget Summary sheet after the Mileage worksheet.
b. Change the header for the *Projected Ticket Sales* section to **Ticket Sales**. Because *Paul's Kitchen* came in on budget, you do not need to make any changes to the budget section.
c. Enter the following ticket sales numbers as your final sales figures, replacing the projected figures:

Ticket Type	At Door Seats	Advance Seats
Senior Citizens	84	252
Adults	163	604
Students	111	72

d. Use the final sales figures to construct two pie charts on this sheet to compare the percentage of ticket types. The first chart should show percentage by ticket type of advance tickets sold. The second chart should show the percentage by ticket type of tickets sold at the door. Position the first chart so the top-left corner is in or near **cell M4** and the second chart should have its top-left corner in or near **cell M23** and size the charts as necessary.
e. Apply **Chart Style 3** to both charts to include chart titles, legends, and data labels showing percentages. Replace the text **Chart Title** with an appropriate title for each chart.
f. Save and close the workbook. Based on your instructor's directions, submit 01e_Theatre_LastFirst.

Production Assistants

Use Microsoft Access

Background

In order to store and analyze the data for a theater company, production assistants might use Microsoft Access. They create and maintain tables, create and edit queries, and create forms and reports. Theater data includes shows, theaters, actors, and casting. Producers and directors will use this data to determine which actors performed in which shows, which theaters were used more frequently, and which shows were profitable.

Skills:

Chapter 1

Back Up, Compact, and Repair an Access File; Edit a Record; Navigate among the Objects in an Access Database; Open an Access File and Work with Content Security; Save the Database; Sort Table Data on One or More Fields; Work with Field Properties

Chapter 2

Create a Multi-table Query; Create a Single-table Query; Create Tables;, Enforce Referential Integrity; Establish Table Relationships; Import an Excel Spreadsheet; Modify a Multi-table Query; Run, Copy, and Modify a Query; Set a Table's Primary Key; Specify Query Criteria for Different Data Types; Use Query Design View

Chapter 3

Add Aggregate Functions to Datasheets and Queries, Create a Calculated Field in a Query, Create a Totals Query with Grouping, Create Expressions with Expression Builder, Format and Save Calculated Results, Perform Date Arithmetic, Use Built-in Functions in Access, Use the Relationships Window, Verify Calculated Results

Chapter 4

Create Forms Using the Form Tool, Create Reports Using the Report Wizard, Identify Control Types in Forms, Identify Control Types in Reports, Modify a Form, Modify a Report, Preview a Report

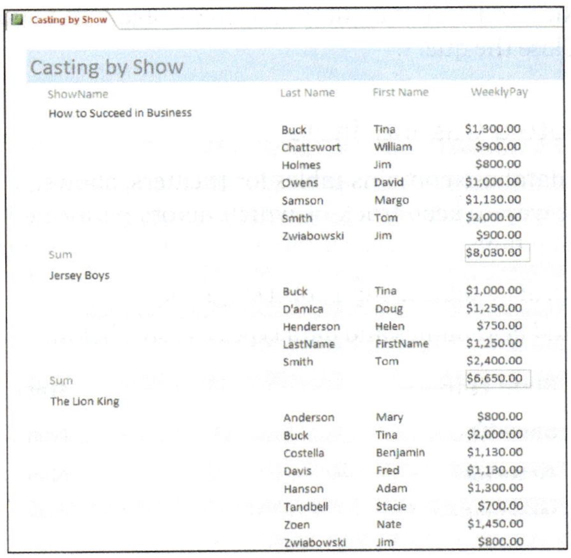

FIGURE 1.3 Production Assistant Database

CASE STUDY | Working as a Production Assistant

Starting Files	Files to be Submitted
01a_Broadway **01a_ImportCasting.xlsx**	**01a_Broadway_LastFirst** **01a_Broadway_LastFirst_yyyy-mm-dd**

Capstone Exercises

You work as a production assistant in the office of the Green Man Theatre. One of your duties is to maintain the company database. You will create and edit tables, queries, forms, and reports as well as maintain and back up the database. A database has already been created, so you decide to explore it.

Navigate among the Objects in an Access Database

You will begin by opening the Broadway database and examining the tables and other objects. You will also make one change in the Actors table.

a. Open the database *01a_Broadway* and save the database as **01a_Broadway_LastFirst**.
b. Open each table and examine the data.
c. Close all the tables except the Actors table.
d. Sort the Actors table by Last Name in ascending order.
e. Find Stacie Henderson's record.
f. Replace the last name *Henderson* with **Tandbell**.
g. Remove the Sort.
h. Save and close the Actors table.
i. Open the *Actors from NY* query.
j. Switch to Design view. Modify the State criterion so the query displays all the actors who are not from NY.
k. Run and save the query (use Save Object As) and rename as **Actors Not from NY**. Close the query.

Create a Casting Table

The database contains tables for theaters, shows, and actors. However, there is no efficient way to keep track of which actors performed in which shows. You will create a Casting table that will contain the show, the actor, and the weekly pay.

a. Create a table using Table Design view.
b. Add field names and data types as listed below.

Field Name	Data Type
ShowID	Number
ActorID	Number
WeeklyPay	Currency

c. Set ShowID and the ActorID together as the primary key.
d. Save the table as **Casting** and close the table.

Import Excel Data into the Casting Table

The theater has been storing casting data in an Excel spreadsheet. You will import this spreadsheet data directly into the Casting table.

a. Append the data in Sheet1 of the *01a_ImportCasting* Excel file into the Casting table. If an error message displays, click Yes.

b. Open the Casting table and examine the data.

c. Verify the primary key is set correctly by changing the last record's ActorID from *12* to **9**. Click the record directly above and Access will display the message *The changes you requested to the table were not successful because they would create duplicate values...* Undo the change to ActorID.

d. Close the table.

Establish Table Relationships

Table relationships help users extract data more efficiently. Referential integrity will help eliminate common data entry mistakes. You will set two new relationships and enforce referential integrity.

a. Open the Relationships window and add the Casting and Actors tables.

b. Set a relationship between the Shows and Casting tables and set Enforce Referential Integrity.

c. Set a relationship between the Actors and Casting tables and set Enforce Referential Integrity.

d. Make sure all table data and join lines are visible.

e. Save and close the Relationships window.

Create a Casting Query

You need to post the casting roll for each new show. You will create a casting roll for the latest show using a query.

a. Create a query based on the Casting table. Include only the ShowID and ActorID fields.

b. Add criteria to display all the actors who performed in ShowID 3, which is *Jersey Boys*.

c. Run the query.

d. Save the query as **Jersey Boys Cast**.

e. Close the query.

Copy and Modify an Existing Query

The previous query does not show the name of the show or the name of the actor. You will copy the previous query and revise it to add the missing data.

a. Copy the Jersey Boys Cast query and paste it using the name **Jersey Boys Cast Enhanced**. Open the Jersey Boys Cast Enhanced query in Design view.

b. Add the Actors and Shows tables into the new query.

c. Modify the query so that the ShowName displays as the first column and the ShowID field does not display in the query results.

d. Replace the ActorID field with the LastName and FirstName fields.

e. Run the query. Verify the accuracy of the data.

f. Save and close the query.

Use a Calculated Field to Forecast Daily Revenue

The producers asked you for the daily estimated revenue for each show, based on a sold-out house. You will create a query and use a calculated field to provide this information.

a. Create a new query based on the Shows and Theaters tables.
b. Include the ShowName, TheaterName, SeatingCapacity, and TicketPrice fields.
c. Save the query as **Estimated Daily Revenue**.
d. Use the Expression Builder to create the DailyRevenue calculated field in the fifth column. Multiply the field SeatingCapacity by TicketPrice to create the calculated field.
e. Close the Expression Builder, run the query, and then manually verify whether the calculated field values are correct.
f. Save and close the query.

Use Functions in a Query

The producers ask you to modify and improve the Estimated Daily Revenue query. You will copy the existing query, rename it, and then add the required changes. The new query will require a Totals query so you can look up the total actors' salaries for each show.

a. Create a Totals query from the Casting table that can be used to look up the total actors' salaries for each show. Add the ShowID and WeeklyPay fields. Use the Total row to group by ShowID and sum the WeeklyPay. Run the query and save the query as **Show Salaries**. Close the query.
b. Copy the Estimated Daily Revenue query and paste it using the name **Estimated Daily Revenue and Expenses**.
c. Modify the *Estimated Daily Revenue and Expenses* query to add a Daily Rent calculated field to the sixth column using **DailyRent: [WeekRentalFee]/7**. Change the format property to **Currency**. Run the query and verify whether the calculated field is working.
d. Switch to **Design view** and add a **Daily Salaries calculated field** to the seventh column using the following expression:

   DailySalaries: DLookUp("SumOfWeeklyPay","Show Salaries","ShowID= " & [ShowID])/7

   The DLookup() function directs Access to look up a value in the Show Salaries query you created in Step a. Change the format property to **Currency**.
e. Run the query and manually verify whether the calculated field values are correct. Save and close the query.
f. Copy the *Estimated Daily Revenue and Expenses* query and paste it using the name **Estimated Net Income**. To the new query, add another calculated field for **DailyNet**. Daily Net is defined as Revenue minus Expenses (DailyRent and DailySalaries). Add another calculated field for **TotalNet**. Total Net is defined as Daily Net times the number of days the show runs. Total Net requires the DateDiff() function, as shown: **TotalNet: [DailyNet]*DateDiff("d",[StartDate],[EndDate]).**
g. Run the query and verify the calculated fields are correct.
h. Save and close the query.

Create a Form Using a Form Tool

You need to create a form to make it easier to add new actors. The same form will function as a maintenance screen for existing actors.

a. Create a form based on the Actors table using the Form tool.
b. Resize the width of the text box controls so they are about half the original size.

c. Remove the subform.
d. Change the title label to **Enter and Edit Actor Data**.
e. Save the form as **Main Actors**.
f. Add yourself as an actor using the new form. Include your real name and make up the rest of the data.
g. Close the form.

Create a Report Using the Report Wizard

You need to create a report that lists all the actors grouped by show. The report should also show the weekly pay for each actor and a sum for each show, as well as display a sum for the weekly pay overall.

a. Create a simple query that will be used to create a report. Include the Casting, Shows, and Actors tables. Add the necessary fields based on the description above.
b. Name the query **Casting Summary**. Close the query.
c. Create a report based on the Casting Summary query using the Report Wizard. Answer the Report Wizard's questions using the description above. Sort by Last Name and name the report **Casting by Show**.
d. Switch to **Layout view** and delete the summary for the ShowName box displayed in the ShowName footer. Preview the report.
e. Switch to **Design view** and move the Sum label and Sum box up to the top of the ShowName footer. Reduce the height of the ShowName footer by one-half. Increase the width of the Grand total field to display the value including the $ sign. Preview the report.
f. Save the report. Close the report.
g. Add yourself as ActorID 20 to the Jersey Boys show with a weekly pay of 1250 in the Casting table and preview the report again.
h. Close the report.

Back Up the Database

An Access database needs to be maintained regularly. As a part of your daily routine, you will back up the database.

a. Back up the database in the location where you save your student files. When naming the file, include today's date.
b. Save and close all open database objects. Based on your instructor's directions, submit 01a_Broadway_LastFirst.

Production Assistants

Use Microsoft PowerPoint

Background

Microsoft PowerPoint can be a powerful tool for use in a theater company's business office. Production assistants use PowerPoint to create presentations, handouts, and scripts for presentations. It is important that a production assistant become familiar with planning a presentation, creating text, inserting media, and working with transitions and animation to utilize the benefits of this program.

Skills:

Chapter 1

Add a Table, Add New Slides, Animate Objects, Apply Transitions, Create a New Presentation, Edit the Title Slide, Insert a Media Object, Reorder Slides, Use PowerPoint Views, Use Slide Layouts, Use Spell Check

Chapter 2

Import an Outline, Reuse Slides from an Existing Presentation

Chapter 3

Apply WordArt to Text, Arrange Objects, Change a Shape Outline, Create SmartArt, Group Objects, Modify Objects, Modify SmartArt, Modify WordArt, Use a Callout Shape

Chapter 4

Add Audio from a File, Apply Themes, Change Audio Settings, Insert a Picture, Remove a Picture Background, Transform a Picture

Konstantin Sutyagin/Shutterstock, Manuel Fernandes/Shutterstock, Simone van den Berg/Shutterstock, Terence Mendoza/Shutterstock; PowerPoint 2016, Windows 10, Microsoft Corporation

FIGURE 1.4 Production Assistant Presentation

CASE STUDY | Working as a Production Assistant

Starting Files	Files to be Submitted
01p_gmlogo.jpg	**01p_Season_LastFirst**
01p_gmaudio.mp3	**01p_Kiosk_LastFirst**
01p_Outline.docx	
01p_Brochure	
01p_Paul's_Kitchen_1.jpg	
01p_Paul's_Kitchen_2.jpg	
01p_Christmas_at_the_Andersons'.jpg	
01p_This_Was_Not_In_The_Brochure.jpg	

Capstone Exercises

You work as a production assistant in the offices of a new company, the Green Man Theatre. You have been asked to create a presentation to display in a kiosk in the theater shop and box office to advertise season tickets.

Create a Title Slide

You create a title slide for the new presentation, and you insert audio to catch the attention of viewers.

a. Create a new PowerPoint slide show using the **Facet theme** and save it as **01p_Season_LastFirst**.
b. Format the background style to apply the **Canvas texture** to this slide and all other slides.
c. Add the title **GREEN MAN THEATRE** in the title placeholder. Select the title and apply WordArt **Gradient Fill: Orange, Accent color 4; Outline – Accent color 4**. Resize the title font to **60 pt**.
d. Type **2018–2019 Season** in the **subtitle field** of the title slide. Change the font to **White, Background 1** and bold. Resize the subtitle font to **40 pt**.
e. Insert the Green Man Theatre logo, *01p_gmlogo.jpg*. Remove the white background from the logo and resize the logo to a height **4.3"**.
f. Position the logo in the top-right corner of the slide.
g. Add the *01p_gmaudio* audio file on Slide 1. Set the playback options to play the audio across slides, hide the icon during the show, and if necessary, Start Automatically. Position the audio icon on the bottom-left corner of the slide.
h. Apply the **Start After Previous animation option** to the audio icon.
i. Apply the following **entrance animations** and review the presentation to ensure the animation is correct:

Object	Animation	Start	Duration	Delay
Title placeholder	Grow & Turn	With Previous	04.00	18.00
Subtitle placeholder	Swivel	With Previous	03.00	03.00
Logo image	Bounce	With Previous	06.00	10.00

Create a Content with Caption Slide

You add a new slide for the mission statement, type content in the placeholders, format the text, and then reposition the placeholders.

a. Insert a new slide using the **Content with Caption layout**.
b. Type **Mission Statement** in the title placeholder and change the font size to **54 pt**.
c. Type **Green Man Theatre** in the text placeholder below the title and change the font color to **Orange, Accent 4**. Change the font size to **32 pt**.

d. Add the following mission statement to the content placeholder:

We are committed to providing the environment and the resources for new artists, musicians, actors, and dancers to create and perform new works in the Twin Cities.

e. Change the font size of the text in the content placeholder to **30 pt**. Adjust the position of the placeholder so that the bullet symbol is aligned across from the title text and remove the bullet formatting.

Create a Title and Content Slide

You insert a new slide, add and format a table, insert a logo, add a callout object, and then apply an animation.

a. Insert a new slide using the **Title and Content layout**. Title it **Green Man Theatre Presents**. Change the title text color to **Orange, Accent 4**.

b. Insert a two-column by four-row table on the slide. Enter the following information:

Show	Dates
Paul's Kitchen	September 9–October 2, 2018
Christmas at the Andersons'	November 25–December 18, 2018
This Was Not in the Brochure	February 23–March 19, 2019

c. Apply the **Light Style 2 – Accent 4 table style** to the table.

d. Copy the logo from the Title slide and paste it on Slide 3. Resize the logo to height **3.45"**. Center-align the logo at the bottom edge of the slide.

e. Insert a **Speech Bubble: Oval Callout shape** to the right of the logo and type **2018–2019 Season** in the callout. Format the callout style to **Colored Outline – Orange, Accent 4**.

f. If necessary, resize the shape to display all the text. Position the callout so it is associated with the logo image and move the callout point so that it appears to come from the logo man's mouth. Group the logo and the callout.

g. Apply a **Float In entrance animation** with **Float Down effects** to the title placeholder, having it start **After Previous**. Copy the animation to the logo group and then to the table.

Add Existing Content to a Presentation

You have an outline describing two of the three plays of the season in a Word file. You also have the start of a slide show about the third play. You use this existing content to add the show descriptions to the presentation you are creating.

a. Use the Slides from Outline feature to add both slides contained in the *01p_Outline* file to the end of 01p_Season_LastFirst.

b. Add a slide at the end of the presentation by reusing the slide in *01p_Brochure.*

c. Use Format Painter to apply the format from the content placeholder on Slide 2 to Slides 4–6 and copy the format from the title on Slide 3 to Slides 4–6.

d. Modify the outline in Outline view by moving the bullets referring to the show running dates so they are the first bullet in each of the new Slides 4–6.

e. Insert the following pictures on the slides:

File	Slide
01p_Paul's_Kitchen_1	4
01p_Paul's_Kitchen_2	4
01p_Christmas_at_the_Andersons'	5
01p_This_Was_Not_in_the_Brochure	6

f. Resize and position the images attractively on the slides.

g. Format each of the photos by removing backgrounds, applying color corrections, adjusting color, applying filters, and/or adding picture styles.

h. Insert a new slide after Slide 6 using the **Content with Caption layout**.

i. Add the title **Season Tickets** and change the font size to **44 pt**. Type **Green Man Theatre** in the content text box below the title and change the font color to **Orange, Accent 4**. Change the font size to **32 pt**.

j. Add these bullets in the content box:

- **Available in the Box Office and Theater Shop**
- **Discount on Season Tickets**
- **Patron Memberships Available**

k. Change the content text size to **32 pt** and apply **12 pt** after to the paragraph spacing.

l. Copy the logo image from the first slide and resize and position the logo below the slide's title.

Create SmartArt

You create a SmartArt diagram to explain the three levels of giving and the amount required to achieve a particular level. Different benefits are available to patrons of different levels.

a. Insert a new slide after Slide 7 using the Title Only layout.

b. Type **Patronage Levels** in the title placeholder and format the text to match the title on Slide 3.

c. Create a **Pyramid List SmartArt** to display three levels of giving.

- Platinum $10,000
- Gold $1,000
- Silver $100

d. Change the color of the SmartArt style to **Colorful Range–Accent Colors 2 to 3**.

e. Apply the **SmartArt 3-D Cartoon style**.

f. Display the slides in Slide Sorter view and move Slide 8 (Patronage Levels) behind Slide 2 (Mission Statement).

Finalize the Presentation

You apply final transitions and animations to the presentation, and then prepare the presentation to play automatically at the kiosk located at the entrance to the theater.

a. Apply the **Reveal transition effect** for all slides.

b. Apply a consistent entrance animation of your choice to all bulleted content placeholders in the presentation. The bullets should enter one by one.

c. Apply an animation to the SmartArt on Slide 3 that wipes the objects from the left and one by one.

d. Apply an animation of your choice to each of the images you inserted on the slides introducing the plays.

e. Check for spelling or grammar errors.

f. View the presentation and make any changes necessary, then save the presentation.

g. Save the presentation again as **01p_Kiosk_LastFirst**.

h. Set up the slide show so it can be browsed at a kiosk. Set the slide show to use slide timings.

i. Use the Rehearse Timings feature to add automatic slide timings to advance each of the slides in the presentation. Use approximately 25 seconds for the first slide and 10 seconds for the other slides.

j. Save and close the file. Based on your instructor's directions, submit 01p_Season_LastFirst and 01p_Kiosk_LastFirst.

Production Assistants

Integrate Microsoft Office Software

Background

Each program in the Microsoft Office suite has its strength and specialty. The theater production office assistant needs to use each software application in the suite for the appropriate task. Microsoft Word is useful to create fliers and brochures for upcoming plays and musicals, letters to send to patrons and donors, and so on. Microsoft Excel is appropriate to store budgets for the current and upcoming productions and to develop schedules and reimbursement forms that require mathematical calculations. Microsoft PowerPoint is beneficial for creating presentations for advertising the productions or when meeting with investors. Microsoft Access is a database management program that provides the capability to store and analyze large quantities of data. At times, the production office assistant needs to use all four programs together to create the desired result. For example, the production assistant may use data from Access to generate an Excel workbook for further data analysis and then create a chart that can then be linked to a PowerPoint presentation shared with the theater board members as a PDF file.

Skills:

Create a Summary Query, Export Query Results to an Excel Worksheet, Group Worksheets, Apply Cell Styles, Calculate Statistics Using Statistical Analysis Functions, Create Charts from Data, Use Quick Analysis to Create a Chart, Display the Statistics and Charts as Linked Objects in a PowerPoint Presentation, Share the Presentation as an Email PDF Attachment

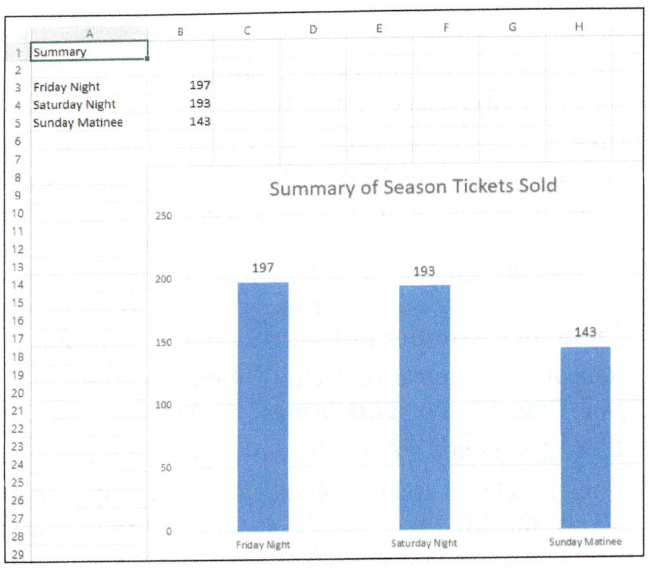

FIGURE 1.5 Production Assistant Documents

CASE STUDY | Working as a Production Assistant

Starting File	Files to be Submitted
01i_SeasonTickets.accdb	**01i_SeasonTickets_LastFirst.accdb** **01i_SeatCount_LastFirst.xlsx** **01i_Stats_LastFirst.pptx**

Capstone Exercises

You work as a production office assistant in the offices for the Green Man Theatre. You maintain the season tickets database. Your job entails creating and executing queries to help the production manager make critical decisions about the theater's operations. At times, you need to export Access data into an Excel worksheet for other data manipulations, create charts in Excel that you can import into a PowerPoint presentation, and import data into Word documents for distribution.

Export Queries to Excel

The sales manager asks you to create a query to determine how many seats each season ticket holder owns for the opening weekend and then import the results into an Excel workbook so he can analyze sales. You will export the tables and a few queries for just the opening weekend to a test database so you do not accidentally change any of the data in the actual database. If this becomes a regular function, you will move the queries into the actual database. Season tickets are sold by the seat. Each show has its own set of seats. The tables of seats for each show are the following:

Table	Show
Show1	Opening Friday Night
Show2	Opening Saturday Night
Show3	Opening Sunday Matinee

a. Open the Access database *01i_SeasonTickets.accdb* and save it as **01i_SeasonTickets_LastFirst**.

b. Create a query for Friday night using the Show1 table and the SeasonTicketHolders table. Insert the fields in the following sequence: CustomerNum from the Show1 table, LastName and FirstName from the SeasonTicketHolders table, and Seat from the Show1 table. Group by CustomerNum and create a calculated field to count the number of seats each ticket holder owns for opening Friday night. Customize the column labels using the Property Sheet to display **Seat Number** instead of *Seat* and **Customer Number** instead of *CustomerNum*. Save the query as **SeatCount1**.

c. Repeat Step b above, replacing Show2 and Show3 for Show1 and naming the queries **SeatCount2** and **SeatCount3**, respectively.

d. Close Access and submit the database based on your instructor's directions.

e. Open Excel and create a blank workbook. Import data from the three queries created above into the Excel workbook. In the **Select Table dialog box**, check the box to enable selection of multiple tables. Next, select the option to view the data as a table in the workbook.

f. Delete Sheet1, which is blank. Rename each worksheet tab with data according to the show number in the last column. For example, Sheet2 will be renamed to *Show1*.

g. Save the Excel workbook as **01i_SeatCount_LastFirst**.

Perform Statistics Calculations on Imported Data in Excel

After you give the workbook to the sales manager, he comes by your office and admits he does not know what to do with it. He asks if you could do some analysis on the buying habits of the season ticket holders. He wants you to create a summary area in which you perform statistical calculations on each worksheet's data. For each show, he wants to know the total number of seats sold and the number of ticket holders, along with the maximum, minimum, and average number of seats purchased by each ticket holder.

a. Set the first sheet, Show1, as the active sheet. Press and hold **Shift** as you click the **Show3 tab** to group the three sheets together.
b. Click **cell H1**, type **Sales Statistics for Opening Friday Night**, and then press **Enter**. Bold the label and apply the **Accent6 cell style**.
c. Click **cell H2** and type the following labels down the column:

   Total seats sold

   Number of ticket holders

   Maximum number of seats purchased

   Minimum number of seats purchased

   Average number of seats purchased
d. Apply **merge and center** to the **range H1:I1**. Adjust the width of column H to best fit the remaining labels.
e. Use Statistical Analysis Functions in column I for each respective label.
f. Select **cell I6**, apply **Comma Style**, and then display one decimal place.
g. Click the second worksheet tab to ungroup the sheets.
h. Review each function on the other two worksheets and adjust the ranges within the function arguments as needed for each particular sheet of data. In **cell H1** for the other two worksheets, replace *Friday Night* with **Saturday Night** and **Sunday Matinee**, respectively.
i. Save the workbook.

Create a Summary Chart

The sales manager wants you to create a column chart that depicts the total number of season tickets sold by opening night. You will consolidate the data on a new worksheet in order to be able to create a column chart.

a. Insert a new worksheet in front of Show1, and name it **Summary**.
b. Type **Summary** in **cell A1** and press **Enter** twice.
c. Type **Friday Night**, **Saturday Night**, and **Sunday Matinee**, respectively, in the **range A3:A5**. Widen the column to fit the data.
d. Click **cell B3**, type =, click the **Show1 sheet tab**, click the cell containing the total seats sold function, and then press **Enter**.
e. Adapt Step d to create formulas that point to the original respective functions for the total seats sold for Saturday and Sunday.
f. Select the Summary data and use Quick Analysis to create a clustered column chart. Add an appropriate chart title, add data labels, and then increase the font size of the data labels to **12 pt**.
g. Move the chart below the data to cover the **range B8:I29**. Click in any cell to deselect the chart.
h. Save the workbook.

Link Data into a PowerPoint Presentation

The sales manager is pleased with the statistical analysis and chart you added to the Excel workbook. He decides to use the summary data and chart in a PowerPoint presentation that he can show at the next board meeting. You will create a presentation with a title slide, the three summary statistical tables on one slide, and the chart on a third slide.

a. Start PowerPoint and select the **Main Event design template**. Apply the green shaded variant to the design. Save the presentation as **01i_Stats_LastFirst**.
b. Type **GREEN MAN THEATRE** in the title placeholder and type **OPENING NIGHT TICKET SALES** in the subtitle placeholder on the title slide.
c. Insert a second slide using the Title Only layout and do the following:
    - Type **SUMMARY STATISTICS PER SHOW** as the title.
    - Copy the Sales Statistics for Opening Friday Night range on the Show1 sheet from the *01i_SeatCount_LastFirst* workbook and use Paste Special to paste a link onto the slide.
    - Copy the Sales Statistics for Opening Saturday Night range on the Show2 sheet from the *01i_SeatCount_LastFirst* workbook below the first linked range on the slide using Paste Special to paste a link onto the slide.
    - Copy the Sales Statistics for Opening Sunday Matinee range on the Show3 sheet from the *01i_SeatCount_LastFirst* workbook below the second linked range on the slide using Paste Special to paste a link onto the slide.
    - Increase the width of each summary area object and arrange them to be centered under the title.
d. Insert a third slide, using the Blank layout. Copy and link the column chart from the workbook onto the slide. Using the top-left corner of the image, drag it toward the top-left edge of the slide to enlarge it, and then apply align center.
e. Save the presentation.

Share the Presentation

Finally, after you prepare the presentation, the sales manager asks you to create a PDF of the presentation to email to the board of directors before the meeting.

a. Use the File Share feature in PowerPoint to email your instructor a PDF attachment of the presentation .pdf now included.
b. Replace the file name with **Green Man Theatre – Summary Statistics_LastFirst** as the email subject.
c. Type a brief message to encourage the recipient to open and review the attached presentation file.
d. Send the email message.
e. Exit all open programs.
f. Based on your instructor's directions, submit:
    01i_SeasonTickets_LastFirst
    01i_SeatCount_LastFirst
    01i_Stats_LastFirst

Business Discipline

DISCIPLINE 2

Using Microsoft Office as a Business Professional

DragonImages/Fotolia

LEARNING OUTCOMES

- **You will use Word, Excel, Access, PowerPoint, and integrated applications in projects specific to the business discipline.**
- **You will use Word to prepare the mailing of the letter inviting shareholders to the annual meeting.**
- **You will use Excel to develop the financial statements for the annual shareholder's meeting.**
- **You will use Access to maintain a database of company information including data about the employees, products, and shareholders.**
- **You will use PowerPoint to create a presentation on motorcycle safety to use for community outreach.**

CASE STUDY | Working as a Business Professional

Your career at Healthy Living Motorcycles, Inc., involves a variety of communication, collaboration, and analytical skills. You are often required to communicate with others through written documents, emailed reports, and presentations. The documents and presentations may be developed by you alone, or by a work group residing across the globe. In many areas of business, you also are called on to organize and analyze data.

The Microsoft Office suite of applications provides tools that are critical in helping the business professionals, from office assistants to CEOs, with whatever task is required. For example, you would use Word to write letters, memos, reports, brochures, or newsletters. With PowerPoint, you can design presentations or even flyers to communicate information to your customers or stakeholders. You could be required to create budgets and to analyze financial or sales data using Excel. Finally, Access can help you to capture and store sales and other customer-related data and then filter and sort that data into meaningful information that can then be used by others in your company.

Business Professionals

Use Microsoft Word

Background

Companies place office managers and directors in charge of various departments, which include accounting, finance, human resources, marketing, manufacturing and production, public relations, and research and development. These upper-management employees are responsible for planning and supervising the work of their subordinates and for achieving the organizational goals so that the company is successful. Office managers use word-processing software on a daily basis to prepare correspondence, record notes, and prepare reports and proposals. Although email and messaging have replaced some written correspondence, office managers still often use word-processing software to prepare written documents.

Skills:

Chapter 1

Check Spelling and Grammar, Format a Footer, Insert a Footer, Insert a Page Break, Insert a Symbol, Insert a Watermark, Modify Document Properties, Modify Paragraph Spacing, Set and Modify Line and Paragraph Spacing, Set Margins

Chapter 2

Apply Styles, Change Document Theme, Create a Multilevel List, Replace an Image, Resize an Image, Use WordArt

Chapter 3

Add a Caption, Complete a Mail Merge, Adjust Row Height, Adjust Table Position and Alignment, Apply a Table Style, Convert Text to a Table, Format Table Text, Insert a Row, Insert Graphics in a Table

Chapter 4

Acknowledge a Source, Add Text to Content Controls on a Cover Page, Create Footnotes, Insert a Cover Page, Use a Data Source, Use Track Changes, View and Delete a Comment

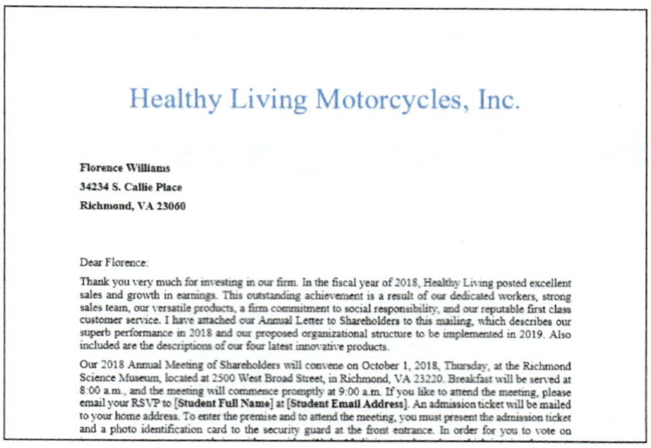

Healthy Living Motorcycles, Inc.

Florence Williams
34234 S. Callie Place
Richmond, VA 23060

Dear Florence:

Thank you very much for investing in our firm. In the fiscal year of 2018, Healthy Living posted excellent sales and growth in earnings. This outstanding achievement is a result of our dedicated workers, strong sales team, our versatile products, a firm commitment to social responsibility, and our reputable first class customer service. I have attached our Annual Letter to Shareholders to this mailing, which describes our superb performance in 2018 and our proposed organizational structure to be implemented in 2019. Also included are the descriptions of our four latest innovative products.

Our 2018 Annual Meeting of Shareholders will convene on October 1, 2018, Thursday, at the Richmond Science Museum, located at 2500 West Broad Street, in Richmond, VA 23220. Breakfast will be served at 8:00 a.m., and the meeting will commence promptly at 9:00 a.m. If you like to attend the meeting, please email your RSVP to **[Student Full Name]** at **[Student Email Address]**. An admission ticket will be mailed to your home address. To enter the premise and to attend the meeting, you must present the admission ticket and a photo identification card to the security guard at the front entrance. In order for you to vote on

Word 2016, Windows 10, Microsoft Corporation

FIGURE 2.1 Working as a Business Professional Document

CASE STUDY | Working as a Business Professional

Starting Files	Files to be Submitted
02w_AnnualLetter	**02w_AnnualLetter_LastFirst**
02w_Bike1.jpg	**02w_CoverLetter_LastFirst**
02w_Bike2.jpg	**02w_MergedLetters_LastFirst**
02w_Bike3.jpg	
02w_Bike4.jpg	
02w_CoverLetter	
02w_Dataset	

Capstone Exercises

You work as the assistant director of the Public Relations department of Healthy Living Motorcycles, Inc. Your company will be holding its annual meeting soon, and you are responsible for mailing the annual letter and accompanying materials to the shareholders. Your executive assistant collected the necessary information and wrote a draft for you. You will review the draft and add your changes and suggestions to the annual letter to shareholders. In addition, you will draft a cover letter to accompany the annual letter and to provide more information about the annual meeting.

Set Initial Document Formats

It is important to format documents to improve readability and to conform to company requirements. You will change the margins, format the characters and spacing, and insert a watermark. You also want the page number and the company name to appear in the footer of every page.

a. Open *02w_AnnualLetter* and save it as **02w_AnnualLetter_LastFirst**.
b. Set the margin setting to **Normal**.
c. Select the entire document and set the paragraph Line spacing option to **Single**, Spacing After option to **6 pt**, Alignment option to **Justified**, and font type and size to **Times New Roman**, **11 pt**.
d. Type the word **DRAFT**as a semitransparent, diagonal watermark.
e. Insert the **Integral style** footer. Type **your full name** in the Author text field. The page number appears after the typed text.
f. Format the footer using **Times New Roman**, **10 pt**.

Insert a Cover Page

You want the document to look professional and eye-catching, so you add a "colorful" image to the cover page to make it more interesting.

a. Insert a cover page at the beginning of the document using the **Integral** design. Replace the image with the *02w_Bike1.jpg* file. Increase the height of the image to **2.5"**.
b. Change the document theme to **Integral**.
c. Change the document title to **Annual Letter**. Change the font to **Times New Roman**, **bold**, and decrease the font by one size.
d. Type **Healthy Living Motorcycles, Inc.** as the document subtitle.
e. Change the abstract title to **To Our Shareholders**. Change the font to **Times New Roman**, **bold**, and increase the font by one size.
f. Type **Our Motto: We are committed to global sustainability and social responsibility.** in the Abstract content control.
g. Change the author's name to **your full name** and the font type to **Times New Roman**. Type **Assistant Director of Public Relations** in the Course content control.

Review a Document Using Track Changes

Your executive assistant added several comments in the document. After reviewing the document, you incorporate the changes in the document and remove all comments and highlighting.

a. Change the Display for Review options to **All Markup** to display all comments.

b. Insert **2018** before the text *Net Sales Performance* as indicated in the second comment.

c. Delete all three comments and change the Display for Review options to No Markup.

Convert Text to a Table and Format Table

Your executive assistant was not sure how to format the net sales information. You decide that putting the sales figures in a table will make it easier for shareholders to understand.

a. Move to the 2018 Net Sales Performance section. Select all the text starting with *Countries* and ending with *-5.8*. Convert the selected text to a table. Use two columns and separate text by tabs. Delete any empty rows. Change the column width of the first column to **1.8"** and the second column to **3"**. Select the whole table and change the row height to **0.3"**.

b. Insert one row at the top of the newly created table. Merge the cells in the new first row. Change the row height to **0.4"**. Cut and paste the text **2018 Net Sales Performance** located above the table into the merged cell. Insert a footnote at the end of the table title with the text: **Source: Healthy Living Annual Report, 2018**. Insert the **copyright symbol** after the year.

c. Apply the **Grid Table 4 - Accent 2 Table Style** to the table.

d. Select the whole table and set the paragraph Spacing After option to **0 pt** and the cell alignment to **Align Center Left**. **Center** the table horizontally on the page.

e. Set the alignment to **Align Center** in the first row.

f. Bold the *2018 Net Sales % Change* column heading in the second row.

g. Indent all the countries under each continent (Asia and Europe) by **0.5"** and sort the countries in ascending order within each continent.

h. **Bold** and **right-align** the total percentages for Asia and Europe.

i. Create a caption to display above the table. Type **A Comparison of Two Years' Sales** as the caption for the table. Center the caption and change the font type to **Times New Roman, 11 pt**.

Insert and Format Graphics

You want to showcase the four new inventions strategically on the third page of the document.

a. Insert a page break right before the *Four Latest Innovative Products* heading.

b. Format the *Four Latest Innovative Products* heading as **Heading 1**. Modify Heading 1's font type to **Times New Roman**, **Bold**, and the paragraph Spacing After option to **12 pt**.

c. Place the insertion point before *Sports Motorcycle # 1* and insert a two-columns-by-two-rows table. Set the cell height to **2.5"** and cell width to **3.25"**.

d. Insert the *02w_Bike1.jpg* image in the cell of row 1 column 1, *02w_Bike2.jpg* in the cell of row 1 column 2, *02w_Bike3.jpg* image in the cell of row 2 column 1, and *02w_Bike4.jpg* in the cell of row 2 column 2.

e. Change the height of all four images to **2"** and set the images to **Align Top Center**.

f. Create a caption for each figure by cutting and pasting the motorcycle information listed in the document and place the caption below the image.

g. Center the captions. Center the table and remove all the borders of the table.

h. Insert a page break to force the paragraph below the graphics onto a new page.

i. Select the text starting with *Chairman, President,* and *CEO to VP - Global Outreach* on the fourth page, and format it as a Multilevel List that uses bullets. Use any bullet images of your own choosing.

j. Apply the Heading 1 style to the *Thank You for Your Support and Faith in Us* heading.

Prepare the Document for Sharing and Change Document Properties

Before sending the final document to your director for her approval, you will check for misspellings, remove widows or orphans, and insert nonbreaking spaces.

a. Use the Spelling & Grammar tool to check the annual letter for errors and correct all misspelled words.

b. Proofread the document and correct any errors you identify.

c. Set the document's advanced properties with the following information (the first three should be set already):

- The Author is **your full name**.
- The Title is **annual letter**.
- The Subject is **Healthy Living Motorcycles, Inc**.
- Keywords are **motorcycles, bikes, sustainability, environmentally-friendly**.

d. Save and close the document.

Modify the Cover Letter and Complete a Mail Merge

Your executive assistant used an existing standard company letter template to write the cover letter, so you simply have to change some of the information in the letter instead of having to create a new one. However, you need to make sure that all personal information, such as names and addresses, is correct. Then you will complete a mail merge.

a. *Open 02w_CoverLetter*, and save it as **02w_CoverLetter_LastFirst**.

b. Format the document as follows:

- Set the margin setting to **Normal**.
- Select the entire document, and set the Line spacing option to **Single**, paragraph Spacing Before and After options to **6pt**, Alignment option to **Justified**, and font type and size to **Times New Roman, 11 pt**.

c. Insert **four** blank lines at the beginning of the document.

d. Use the **WordArt Fill - Blue, Accent 1, Shadow style, font size 28** to insert **Healthy Living Motorcycles, Inc.**, and center it across the top of the letter.

e. Start a Mail Merge using the Step-by-Step Mail Merge Wizard. Use the current letter as the starting document, and the recipient information is derived from *02w_Dataset*.

f. Replace the bracketed placeholders in the letter, *Address Block, First Name*, and *Email Address*, with fields from the data source. Use default settings for the Address block. Set the paragraph Spacing After for Address Block to **0 pt**.

g. Replace the bracketed placeholders in the letter, *Student Full Name* and *Student Email Address*, with your own full name and email address.

h. Complete the merge, merging all records with the data source, resulting in three letters. Save the merged letters as **02w_MergedLetters_LastFirst**.

i. Ensure that each letter prints on one page. Save and close the documents.

j. Based on your instructor's directions, submit the following:

02w_AnnualLetter_LastFirst
02w_CoverLetter_LastFirst
02w_MergedLetters_LastFirst

Business Professionals

Use Microsoft Excel

Background

Employees in the Accounting and Finance departments find worksheet software such as Microsoft Office Excel indispensable. Worksheets give employees the ability to manipulate data to prepare budgets and financial statements. This is particularly useful in "what-if" analysis, where a change in one number in the worksheet can result in updates to all formulas associated with that specified cell reference.

Skills:

Chapter 1

Adjust Column Width, Apply Alignment and Font Options, Apply Cell Styles, Apply Number Formats, Change Tab Color, Copy a Worksheet, Copy Formulas with AutoFill, Create a Footer, Design a Worksheet, Display Cell Formulas, Enter and Edit Cell Data, Hide Columns and Rows, Insert a Date Function, Insert an Image into a Cell, Insert Columns and Rows, Merge and Center Labels, Rename a Worksheet, Set Margin Options, Set Page Orientation

Chapter 2

Use AutoSum, Use Cell References in a Formula, Use Relative and Absolute Cell References, Use the PMT Function, Use the VLOOKUP Function

Chapter 3

Apply a Chart Layout and a Chart Style, Create Column and Pie Charts, Format Data Labels, Insert Sparklines, Move a Chart, Select a Range and Assign a Name, Select the Data Source, Use a Range

Chapter 4

Apply a Table Style, Apply Conditional Formatting, Create a Table

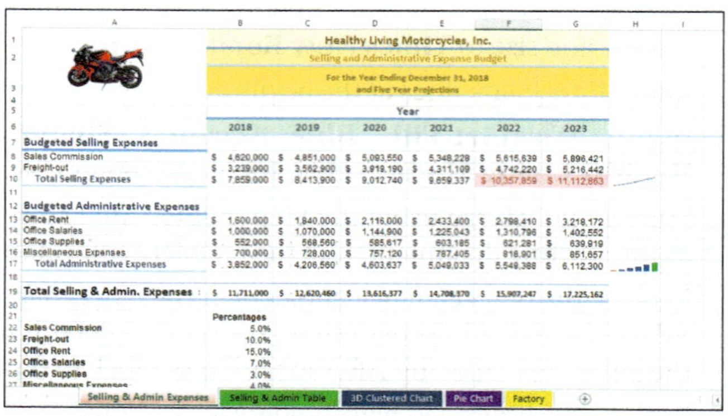

md3d/Fotolia; Excel 2016, Windows 10, Microsoft Corporation

FIGURE 2.2 Working as a Business Professional Worksheet

CASE STUDY | Working as a Business Professional

Starting Files	Files to be Submitted
02e_Budget	**02e_Budget_LastFirst**
02e_Image1.jpg	

Capstone Exercises

You are the assistant director of the Accounting and Finance departments at Healthy Living Motorcycles, Inc. In addition to ensuring that all daily business transactions are completed accurately, you also play a key role in assembling the annual financial reports. Currently, you are responsible for putting together the financial statements to be presented to the upcoming annual stockholders meeting.

Enter and Format Identifying Information

Your executive assistant has collected all the financial statements from the various departments and assembled them into a basic workbook. You will expand on the workbook to include information that would be helpful to you. To give it a professional look, you insert the company image and format the company information at the top of the worksheet. To keep track of the changes, you add your name and the date at the bottom of the worksheet.

a. Open *02e_Budget* and save it as **02e_Budget_LastFirst**.

b. Rename the first worksheet to **Selling & Admin Expenses** and change the worksheet tab color to **Red**.

c. Change the font to **Arial** for the entire worksheet.

d. Insert a blank row below Total Selling Expenses (row 10) and below Total Administrative Expenses (row 17). Use an appropriate date function in **cell A29** to display today's date in your worksheet. Use the **Short Date format**, apply **bold**, and set the font size to **12 pt**. Apply **bold** to the labels in cells B21 and A22:A27.

e. Type your first name and last name in **cell A30**.

f. Create a footer with your **full name** on the left side, the **Sheet Name** in the center, and the **File Name** on the right side of the worksheet.

Format Column Labels and Data

To make the worksheet look more professional, you want to format the column labels and widths.

a. Move the content in **cells A1:A3** to **B1:B3**. Merge the **range A1:A3** and insert *02e_Image1.jpg* into the merged cell. Adjust the height of the image to **1"** and center it in the cell.

b. Merge, center, and apply the **Heading 1 Cell Style** to the **range B1:G1**. Increase the font size by **1**. Select the **Gold, Accent 4, Darker 50% font color**. Apply the **Gold, Accent 4, Lighter 80% fill color**.

c. Merge, center, and apply the **Heading 2 Cell Style** to the **range B2:G2**. Increase the font size by **1**. Select the **Gold, Accent 4, Darker 25% font color**. Apply the **Gold, Accent 4, Lighter 60% fill color**.

d. Merge, center, and apply the **Heading 3 Cell Style** to the **range B3:G3**. Type **and Five Year Projections** on the next line. Increase the font size by **1**. Select the **Gold, Accent 4, Darker 50% font color**. Apply the **Gold, Accent 4, Lighter 40% fill color**.

e. Merge, center, and apply the **Heading 1 Cell Style** to the **range B5:G5**.

f. Apply **Heading 2 Cell Styles** to the **range B6:G6**. Increase the font size to **14 pt**.

g. Apply the **Total Cell Styles** to **range A19:G19**. Increase the font size for **cell A19** to **16 pt**. Change column width of Column A to **41**.
h. Apply **Heading 1 Cell Styles** to **cells A7** and **A12**.
i. Apply **Heading 2 Cell Styles** to **cells A10** and **A17**. Indent both headings **3 times**.
j. Format the **range B8:G19** with **Accounting Number Format with no decimal places**.
k. Format the **range B22:B27** with **Percentage** and **one decimal place**.
l. Ensure all headings are visibly displayed by adjusting all row heights as needed.

Use AutoSum and Absolute References

Employees frequently need summarized information to make good business decisions and future projections. You also want to apply conditional formatting to emphasize values above the average value.

a. Use **AutoSum** for the year of 2018 to find the total selling expenses in **cell B10** and the total administrative expenses in **cell B17**.
b. Create a formula in **cell B19** that adds the total selling and administrative expenses.
c. Use both **absolute references** and **relative references** to reflect the percentages in **range A22:B27** to determine the projected expenses for each of the Budgeted Selling and Budgeted Administrative Expenses for the year of **2019**.
d. Use AutoFill to complete the series in **ranges C8:G17** and **C19:G19**. Ensure all columns are wide enough to display all data fully.
e. Apply the **Light Red Fill with Dark Red Text conditional formatting** to values in the Total Selling Expenses row when the values are more than $10 million.

Assign a Range Name and Use a VLOOKUP and PMT Function

Next, you will proceed to create a range name and insert financial functions into the worksheet. Due to the expansion into the global markets, the board of directors is considering the purchase of a new factory. The board would like to consider the options of financing the purchase over a period of 5 to 40 years, depending on the interest rates and monthly payments. You will present various financing options to the board. The terms and corresponding interest rates are stored in a lookup table. You will assign a range name to the lookup table so that you can use the range name in a function. You will then use the VLOOKUP and PMT functions to determine the monthly payment for the purchase.

a. Assign the range name **Rates** to the **range D2: E10** on the Factory worksheet. Change the worksheet tab color of the worksheet to **yellow**.
b. Create a VLOOKUP function in **cell B6** that looks up the loan period in **cell B5**, compares it to the Rates Lookup table, and then returns the corresponding interest rate. Use the range name for the VLOOKUP function. Change the loan period to perform several "what if" analyses to determine the interest rates for the corresponding loan terms.
c. Create the **PMT** function in **cell B7** to determine the monthly payment based on the financed amount, the loan period, and the corresponding interest rate in **range B4:B6**. Ensure that the monthly payment is a positive number.
d. Format the **Capital Investment** and **Monthly Payment** as **currency with no decimal places**, and all the **Interest Rates** as **percentage with 2 decimal places**. Apply **Top and Double Bottom border** to **cell B7**.

Create Sparklines and Insert a Chart

Executives are very busy and often prefer to view summarized data using charts. You use a column chart to illustrate the projected selling and administrative expenses for the next five years, but you also insert sparklines to display spending trends for the total selling and administrative expenses. Finally, you use a pie chart to compare the percentages of the various expenses for 2018.

a. Select the Selling & Admin Expenses worksheet. Create a 3D Clustered Column chart in a new worksheet based on the **ranges A6:G6, A8:G9**, and **A13:G16** for the 2018 and five years' projections.

b. Apply the **Layout 5 Chart Style** to the column chart to display the data table at the bottom on the chart. Insert the chart title as **Five Years' Projection**. Apply **bold** and increase the chart title font size to **28**.

c. Move the worksheet tab with the 3D Clustered Chart to the right of the Selling & Admin Expenses worksheet tab. Name this worksheet tab **3D Clustered Chart** and change the worksheet tab color to **Blue, Accent 1, Darker, 50%**.

d. Click the **Selling & Admin Expenses worksheet tab** and insert a Line sparkline in **cell H10** for the total selling expenses and a Column sparkline in **cell H17** for the total administrative expenses. Customize the Marker Color for both low points in **red** and the high point in **green**.

e. Create a 2D pie chart for the year 2018 using the labels and data in **ranges A8:B9 and A13:B16**.

f. Move the chart to a new chart sheet named **Pie Chart**, and to the right of the **3D Clustered Chart** sheet. Change the worksheet tab color of the Pie Chart sheet to **Purple**.

g. Type the chart title as **2018 Selling and Administrative Expenses**. Apply the **Style 9 Chart Style** to the pie chart to display the percentages and category names outside each slice. Increase the chart title font size to **20**.

h. Explode the largest slice and insert a block arrow with the text **This is the largest expense** pointing to the largest section of the pie chart. Resize the block arrow to display the whole text.

Create and Format a Table

You want to convert the data in the Selling & Admin Expense worksheet to a table and use Excel's table features to continue working with the data. Since you also want to preserve the original worksheet, you will first create a copy of the worksheet. After you convert a copied data set to a table, you will format it with a table style. You also want to *hide* one column and freeze the column labels so that they do not scroll off screen.

a. Copy the Selling & Admin Expenses worksheet and place the copy after the original worksheet. Rename the copied sheet as **Selling & Admin Table**. Change the worksheet tab color of the new worksheet to **Green**.

b. Select the **range A6:G19**, and convert the data to a table.

c. Remove the conditional formatting rule. Remove sparklines. Apply **Table Style Light 21 table style**.

d. Apply **Green, Accent 6, Darker 50% font color** to the **range B6:G6** to coordinate the font color with the table color. Center all entries.

e. Hide **Column B** (2018) to display only five years' projection.

f. Display the formulas to ensure that all formulas are correct. Protect the current sheet without a password, allowing users to select locked and unlocked cells.

Format and Save the Workbook

a. Review the workbook.

b. Change the orientation for the Selling & Admin Expenses and Selling & Admin Table worksheets to **landscape**. To fit the Selling & Admin Expenses worksheet to one page, change the margins to **Narrow**, the bottom margin to **.5"**, and the width of Column A to **38**. Preview the workbook to make sure that all the individual worksheets fill a single page. Use Page Setup to fit Selling & Admin Table worksheet to one page.

c. Save and close the workbook. Based on your instructor's directions, submit 02e_Budget_LastFirst.

Business Professionals

Use Microsoft Access

Background

Employees use database management software such as Access to maintain and manipulate data for business reasons. The Information Systems (IS) department is primarily responsible for creating and maintaining the databases to be used by all employees in the organization. Database software enables the employees to manipulate data to provide output needed to prepare reports and correspondences.

Skills:

Chapter 1

Add Records, Back Up, Compact, and Repair Access Files, Create a Database, Create and Modify Tables, Design a Table, Navigate among the Objects in an Access Database, Sort Table Data on One or More Fields, Use a Filter

Chapter 2

Create a Multi-table Query, Create a Single-table Query, Enforce Referential Integrity and Assign a Primary Key, Import an Excel Worksheet, Modify a Multi-table Query, Run, Copy, and Modify a Query, Specify Criteria in a Query for Different Data Types, Understand and Establish Table Relationships, Understand Relational Power, Use Built-in Functions in Access, Use Query Design View, Use the Relationships Window

Chapter 3

Create a Calculated Field in a Query, Create a Totals Query with Grouping, Create Expressions with the Expression Builder, Format and Save Calculated Results, Verify Calculated Results

Chapter 4

Change Column Width in Report, Create a Form Using Form Tools, Create Reports Using the Report Wizard, Enter Data in Form View, Modify a Form, Modify a Report, Preview Reports in Print Preview, Revise Reports Using Layout and Design Views

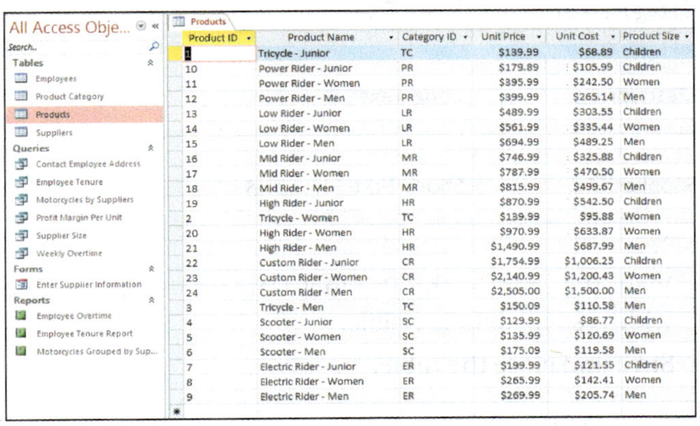

Access 2016, Windows 10, Microsoft Corporation

FIGURE 2.3 Working as a Business Professional Database

CASE STUDY | Working as a Business Professional

Starting Files	Files to be Submitted
02a_Motorcycles **02a_ProductCategory.xlsx**	**02a_Motorcycles_LastFirst**

Capstone Exercises

You are the assistant director for the Information Technology (IT) department at Healthy Living Motorcycles, Inc. In addition to overseeing hardware and software selection, system maintenance, and employee IT training, you create and maintain databases for the whole organization. The organization uses one central database rather than maintaining several individual ones to reduce data redundancy and errors. You will take the opportunity to create an efficient database to keep track of and manage information regarding the company's employees, products, and shareholders.

Create a Table and Import Excel Data

You have an existing database that contains the products sold by the company. However, you need to create a table that will classify each product under a specific category. After the table is created, you import the category data into the new table.

a. Open the *02a_Motorcycles* file and save it as **02a_Motorcycles_LastFirst**

b. Import the data in the *02a_ProductCategory.xlsx* Excel file into a new table. Use the column headings from the Excel file, select the CategoryID field as the primary key, and then save the table as **Product Category**.

c. Ensure the field properties of the Product Category table have been modified as follows:

Field Name	Data Type	Field Size	Comments
CategoryID	Short Text	2	• Assigned a 2-letter code • Caption = Category ID • This is a required field • Set Indexed = Yes (No Duplicates) • Primary key
CategoryName	Short Text	25	• Caption = Category Name • This is a required field • Set Indexed = Yes (No Duplicates)
Description	Long Text		
SupplierID	Short Text	4	• Caption = Supplier ID • All Supplier ID must begin with an "S" • Set Indexed = No

d. View the data in the Product Category table in Datasheet view and adjust column widths so all data is visible.

e. Save and close the table.

Create Relationships

You are now ready to create relationships among the four tables (Employees, Product Category, Suppliers, and Products) so that you can make the database more efficient.

a. Create the following relationships and enforce referential integrity:

- Product Category and Suppliers tables using the SupplierID field
- Suppliers and Employees tables using the EmployeeContactID and EmployeeID fields
- Product Category and Products tables using the CategoryID field

b. Save and close the Relationships window.

Create Filters

You need to quickly find the products that were supplied by a foreign country. You will open the Suppliers table and filter the records.

a. Open the Suppliers table in Datasheet view.

b. Filter the records for the suppliers who were outside of the United States. You should have 11 records.

c. Close the table.

Create a Single-Table Query

The director of marketing has requested a list of the suppliers that have a capacity of more than 25,000 square feet for manufacturing and warehouse space.

a. Create a query using the Suppliers table to display the SupplierID, SupplierName, and Capacity fields for those plants with more than 25,000 square feet. Sort the results by SupplierName in ascending order.

b. Run the query.

c. Name the query as **Supplier Size**.

d. Save and close the query.

Create a Multitable Query

The director of marketing wants a list of the employees who are the main contact with the suppliers. He also wants the addresses of these contact employees so that he can personally send them a letter thanking them for working diligently with these suppliers.

a. Create a query using the Suppliers and Employees tables.

- Display the SupplierName, EmployeeLastName, EmployeeFirstName, E_StreetAddress, E_City, E_State, and E_PostalCode fields. Sort the results by EmployeeLastName, in ascending order.

b. Run the query.

c. Save the query as **Contact Employee Address**.

d. Close the query.

Create a Query and a Date Arithmetic Calculated Field

The human resources manager would like a list of all employees and the approximate length of time they have worked for the company.

a. Create a query using the Employees table and include the EmployeeLastName, EmployeeFirstName, and Date_of_Hire fields.

b. Create an expression in the first blank column of the query that calculates the number of years employees have worked for the company, using the Date_of_Hire field and the current date. Do not adjust for days off. Name the expression **Tenure**. Format the Tenure field as **Fixed with 2 decimal places**.

c. Name the query as **Employee Tenure**.

d. Create a report from the Employee Tenure query.

- Group by Date_of_Hire_by_Month.
- Sort ascending by Date_of_Hire.
- Change the title to **Employee Tenure Report**. Make sure all fields display appropriately.

e. Widen the columns to display all text. Save the report with the default name and close it.

Create a Query with a Profit Margin Calculated Field

The accounting manager works on the income statements and balance sheets, and he would like to know the profit margin for each product.

a. Create a query named **Profit Margin Per Unit**
   - Add ProductName, UnitPrice, and UnitCost fields from the Products table.

b. Use the Expression Builder in the first blank column of the query to create a calculated field named Profit Margin to determine the profit margin for each unit.

c. Format the UnitPrice, UnitCost, and Profit Margin Per Unit fields as **Currency with 2 decimal places**.

d. Sort the query so that the highest profit margins are displayed at the top of the query. Run the query.

e. Find the averages for the UnitPrice, UnitCost, and Profit Margin columns.

f. Save and close the query.

Create a Supplier Form

Your organization is always looking for more suppliers to manufacture products. You create a new form to make it easier to enter new supplier information.

a. Create a new form based on the Suppliers table using the Form tool.

b. Change the title label control to **Enter Supplier Information**.

c. Reduce the text box widths to one-half of their original size.

d. Change the form's control padding to **Narrow**.

e. Save the form as **Enter Supplier Information**.

f. Switch to Form view. Enter a new supplier record, **#15**, using the following information:
   - SupplierID: **S115**
   - SupplierName: **Student's University**
   - Delete the content in EmployeeContactID.
   - Supplier Contact Last Name: **Student Last Name**
   - Supplier Contact Title: **Student**
   - S_StreetAddress, S_City, S_State, S_Postal Code: **Student's school address**
   - S_Country: **USA**
   - Leave Capacity at 0. Leave the Home Page, ProductID, S_Phone, and S_Fax fields blank.

g. Sort the form by SupplierName, ascending order.

h. Save and close the form.

Create a Report Using the Report Wizard

The director of marketing would like a report that lists the suppliers who manufacture the various motorcycles. You create a query and the report for him using the Report Wizard.

a. Create a query and name it **Motorcycles by Suppliers**.
   - Add the SupplierName, SupplierContactLastName, and Capacity fields from the Suppliers table.
   - Add the ProductName and ProductSize fields from the Products table.
   - Add the Product Category table.
   - Sort in descending order by Capacity, but do not display the field in the report.
   - Run, save, and close the query.

b. Create a report based on the **Motorcycles by Suppliers** query.
   - View the data by Suppliers, and group the data by SupplierName.
   - Sort the data by ProductName, ascending order.
   - Select **Landscape Orientation** for the report.
   - Use **Block** layout.
   - Save the report title as **Motorcycles Grouped by Suppliers**.
   - Preview the report.

c. Change the column widths so all the data is visible. Ensure the Report Header title control is wide enough so the entire title is visible. Preview the report.

d. Switch to Print Preview and make sure that the report is displayed on one page. Exit Print Preview and close the report.

Create a Query and a Report with an Overtime Calculated Field

The director of accounting wants to know the cost of time-and-a-half overtime, over and above the regular payroll, for all hourly employees in the organization. You will create a query to find all the employees who worked overtime and create a report based on the query results.

a. Create a query using the Employees table to calculate the hourly rate at time and a half for those employees who work more than 40 hours per week.
   - Include the following fields: EmployeeFirstName, EmployeeLastName, Hours, Rate, and E_State.
   - Calculate the weekly overtime costs in a column called **Weekly Overtime**. Please note: Only the hours worked over 40 hours per week count toward overtime pay. Format the field as **Currency with 2 decimal places**.

b. Name and save the query as **Weekly Overtime**.

c. Create a report for the Weekly Overtime query.
   - Format the report with a title of **Employee Overtime** and all columns fit on one portrait layout page.
   - Switch to Layout view and use the SUM function to calculate the total cost of overtime pay to all employees.
   - Apply the **Organic theme** to the report.
   - Change the report title to **Employee Weekly Overtime**, format the title in **bold.** **Ensure the** Control Margins is set to **None**.

d. Preview the report and adjust column widths so that the content appears on one page.

e. Save the report as **Employee Overtime** and close the report.

Compact, Repair, and Back Up the Database

You compact the database to eliminate any unused space. You also back up the database and save it as another name.

a. Compact and repair the database.

b. Back up the database in the location where you save your student files. When naming the file, include today's date.

c. Based on your instructor's directions, submit 02a_Motorcycles_LastFirst.

Business Professionals

Use Microsoft PowerPoint

Background

Employees of business organizations use presentation software frequently to communicate with others on important topics. Microsoft PowerPoint makes it possible for the user to create presentations with media elements, charts and graphs, and transitions and animations. However, business employees must understand the features of PowerPoint and be comfortable using those features.

Skills:

Chapter 1

Add a Table, Add New Slides, Add Speaker Notes, Create a New Presentation, Format a Table, Run and Navigate a Slide Show, Save Presentation as a PowerPoint Show, Use Slide Layouts, Use Transitions and Animations

Chapter 2

Add a Graphic Image, Import an Outline and Reuse Slides, Modify an Outline in Word

Chapter 3

Create SmartArt, Format Text as WordArt

Chapter 4

Apply Themes, Insert a Video Clip, Insert an Audio Clip, Insert Images, Resize and Apply Picture Effects to Images, Use the Internet as a Resource

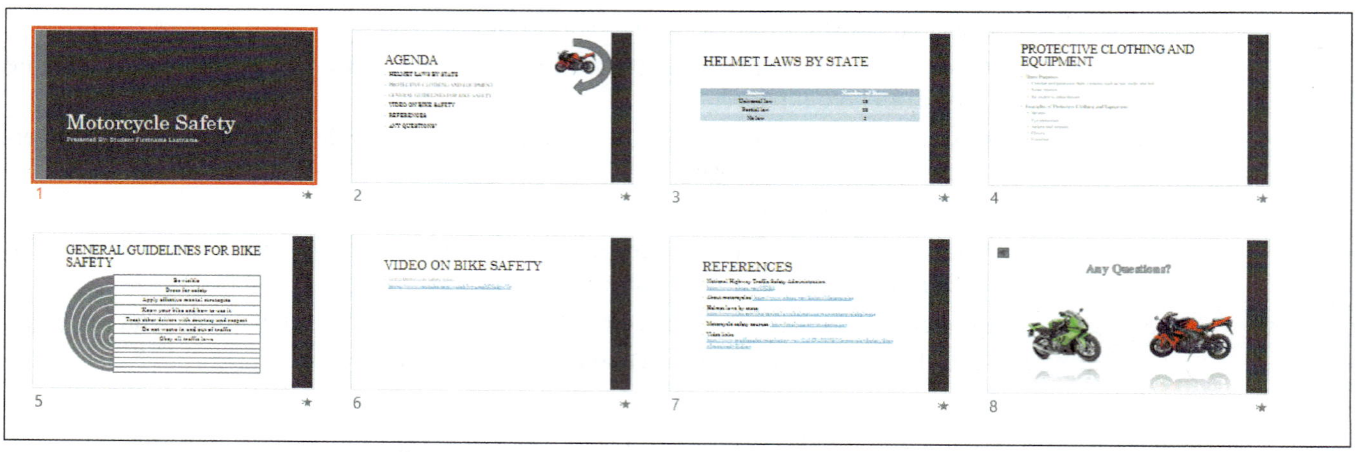

FIGURE 2.4 Working as a Business Professional Presentation

CASE STUDY | Working as a Business Professional

Starting Files	Files to be Submitted
02p_BusOutline.docx	**02p_BusOutline_LastFirst.docx**
02p_Draft	**02p_MotorcycleSafety_LastFirst**
02p_Figure1.jpg	**02p_MotorcycleSafety_LastFirst.ppsx**
02p_Figure2.jpg	

Capstone Exercises

You are the executive assistant to the director of the Public Relations department at Healthy Living Motorcycles, Inc. As an outreach to the community, the director has been asked to present to a local high school about motorcycle safety next week. He would like to educate students on how to stay safe on the roads, and he asked you to prepare the motorcycle safety PowerPoint slide show according to the following instructions.

Modify an Outline in Word

Your director has written an outline for the presentation in Microsoft Word and saved it as a .docx file. You modify the outline before inserting it into a blank presentation.

a. Open the *02p_BusOutline.docx* file in Word and save it as **02p_BusOutline_LastFirst.docx**.
b. Add **AGENDA** as a Heading 1 style at the top of the document and then go to the end of the document and add **ANY QUESTIONS?** as the last Heading 1 style in the document.
c. Save and close the file.

Set Up the Slide Show

You create a presentation using a template, set up the title page, insert a header and footer, and apply a new theme to the document.

a. Start PowerPoint, and create a new presentation using the **Slice** template. Save the presentation as **02p_MotorcycleSafety_LastFirst**.
b. Enter the following text into the placeholders:
   Title placeholder: **Motorcycle Safety**.
   Subtitle placeholder: **Presented By: Student Firstname Lastname**.
c. Create a handout header with your name and a handout footer with your instructor's name and your class. Include the current date.
d. Change the theme to **View**.

Import an Outline and Reuse Slides

Now you are ready to work on the content of the presentation. You import the Word outline into the presentation. Your director also created a basic slide show with speaker notes about motorcycle safety. For efficiency, you reuse this content in your slide show too.

a. Import the *02p_BusOutline_LastFirst.docx* outline file into the presentation.
b. Add the following items at the end of the existing bullets on Slide 4:
   Treat other drivers with courtesy and respect
   Do not weave in and out of traffic
   Obey all traffic laws
c. Select the bullets and apply the **Target List** style in the Relationship SmartArt gallery.
d. Reuse Slides 1 through 3 from *02p_Draft* to add 3 new slides to the presentation after Slide 4. Do not keep the source formatting.
e. Click Slide 5 and copy the speaker note to the Title Slide. Then delete Slide 5.

Insert Images and a Table

Although the slides contain important information, they look bland and boring. To make your presentation more appealing to your audience, you decide to add a few images. You also add a new slide with a table that emphasizes some important facts.

a. Click Slide 7 and change its layout to Two Content. Insert the image *02p_Figure1.jpg* in the left placeholder and *02p_Figure2.jpg* in the right placeholder.

b. Change the width of the images to **3"**. Position the left image at **1.38"** horizontally from the top left corner and **3.22"** vertically from the top left corner. Position the right image at **7.51"** horizontally from the top left corner and **3.22"** vertically from the top left corner.

c. Apply the following Picture Effects to the images:

   Tight Reflection, touching Reflection style to Figure 1.

   Half Reflection, touching Reflection style to Figure 2.

d. Insert a new Slide 3 with the Title and Content layout. Type **HELMET LAWS BY STATE** in the title placeholder. Insert a table with two columns and four rows in the content placeholder.

e. Enter the following information into the table cells:

   Row 1: **Status, Number of States**

   Row 2: **Universal law, 19**

   Row 3: **Partial law, 28**

   Row 4: **No law, 3**

   Center all cell content horizontally and vertically. Apply the **Themed Style 1 – Accent 2** table style. Resize the table to a width of **10.5"** and position it attractively in the blank space.

f. Type **Not all states require riders to wear helmets. Universal law means that all motorcycle riders must wear helmets, while Partial law means only some riders are required to wear helmets.** as a speaker note.

Add a Graphic Shape

Sometimes a graphic shape can be used to draw attention to a topic. You add WordArt and shapes to two slides to enhance the presentation. After adding the shape, you group it with another image to form an attention-grabbing graphic.

a. Click Slide 2. Insert the **Arrow: CircularBlock Arrow shape** (third row, third column in the *Block Arrow category*).

b. Change the width of the shape to **3"** and the height to **4"**.

c. Rotate the arrow to the right **90°**. **Ensure** the arrow head points toward the text placeholder. Position the arrow horizontally at **8.59"** from the top left corner and vertically **–0.08"** from the top left corner.

d. Insert the image *02p_Figure2.jpg*. Position it on top of the Arrow: Circular and send it backward. **Group** the motorcycle image and the Arrow: Circular shape.

e. Click Slide 8. Highlight the *Any Questions?* text, format it with the **Pattern Fill: Gray, Accent color 1, 50%; Hard Shadow: Gray, Accent color 1**, and then center the WordArt in the placeholder.

Modify the Outline and Change Slide Layouts

To focus on the content of the presentation, you review the text in Outline view. You use the spelling checker and make the necessary corrections. You hyperlink the URLs and modify the last slide.

a. Change to Outline view. Review the outline and remove any unnecessary blank lines in the outline. Check the spelling and correct any misspelled words.

b. Switch to Normal view and click **Slide 7**. Format all references as bullets. Then create hyperlinks from the URLs.

c. Copy and paste the slide titles on **Slides 3 – 8** as bullets onto Slide 2 Agenda to finalize the presentation. Use the Format Painter and Change Case so that the last bullet matches the others.

Add Media Objects and Sound

You decide to use the Internet to search for a video clip to add to the presentation to catch the audience's attention. Then you end the presentation with audio.

a. Click **Slide 6**. Insert an Online Video and search YouTube using the keywords *motorcycle safety*.

b. Select an appropriate video clip. Copy and paste the name and URL of the selected video clip onto the text placeholder on Slide 6. Type a short speaker note on this slide about your video.

c. Click Slide 8. Insert **Action Button: Sound**. Set it to play the **Applause sound** on mouse click to signify the end of the presentation. Size to **0.5"** by **0.5"**. Position the button horizontally at **0.39"** from the top left corner and vertically at **0.4"** from the top left corner.

Add Animations and Transitions

The presentation will be shown at high schools to instill good safety habits for newly licensed drivers. You will add animations to introduce elements at appropriate times and to capture the interest of the young audience.

a. Click **Slide 2**. Apply the **Entrance Fly In animation to the bullets**. Set the timing to **After Previous** with a delay and duration of **01.00** second.

b. Click **Slide 4**. Apply the **Entrance Float In animation** and the **Float Down Effect Options** to the first set of bullets. Then apply the **Entrance Float In animation** and the **Float Up Effect Options** to the second set of bullets. Set both animations to start **After Previous** with a duration of **01.00**.

c. Click **Slide 1**. Apply the **Entrance Bounce animation** to the subtitle. Set the animation to start **With Previous** with a duration of **02.00**.

d. Apply **Push** transition effect to odd-numbered slides and **Morph** transition effect to even-numbered slides.

e. View the slide show to ensure the transitions and animations display as intended.

Create a PowerPoint Show, Save, and Close the Presentation

Your director would like to distribute a copy of the presentation outline and make the presentation available online for students who are not able to attend the presentation. Save and close the presentation.

a. Save the *02p_MotorcycleSafety_LastFirst* presentation.

b. Save the presentation again as a PowerPoint Show (*.ppsx).

c. Based on your instructor's directions, submit the following:

   02p_BusOutline_LastFirst.docx

   02p_MotorcycleSafety_LastFirst

   02p_MotorcycleSafety_LastFirst.ppsx

Business Professionals

Integrate Microsoft Office Software

Background

Each program in the Microsoft Office suite has its strength and specialty. Microsoft Word is a word processor used to create documents, such as letters, flyers, and reports. Microsoft Excel is a spreadsheet application used for extensive calculations of data sets. Microsoft PowerPoint is a presentation program that enables users to create unique and professional-looking presentations with animations and transitions. Microsoft Access is a database management program that is perfect for storing and analyzing company data collected over several years. Often, employees will use some or all four programs together while working on a comprehensive project.

Skills:

Import an Excel Worksheet into Access, Create and Utilize a Database Containing Contact Information, Use the Input Mask Wizard, Export an Excel Worksheet from Access, Format a Worksheet, Create Formulas Using Cell References and Absolute References, Apply Theme, Rename Worksheet, Change Tab Color, Merge and Center Labels, Apply Cell Styles, Insert a Date Function, Create a Footer, Create a Chart in Excel, Apply a Chart Style, Use WordArt, Set Page Orientation, Set Margin Options, Insert Watermark, Create Sections in Word, Apply and Modify Headings, Insert a Worksheet into a Word Document; Insert a Footnote, Footer, and Hyperlinks; Complete a Mail Merge, Use a Data Source, Create a Presentation File, Import an Outline, Format Slides, Insert and Format a Chart, Add Animation, Create a PowerPoint Show

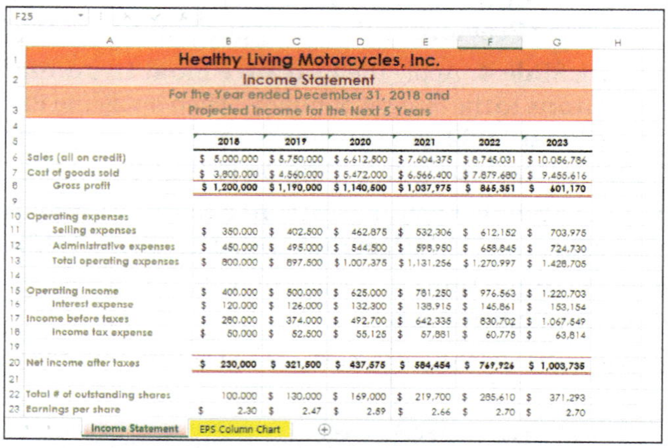

Excel 2016, Windows 10, Microsoft Corporation

FIGURE 2.5 Working as a Business Professional Workbook

CASE STUDY | Working as a Business Professional

Starting Files	Files to be Submitted
02i_HealthyLiving.accdb	02i_HealthyLiving_LastFirst.accdb
02i_IncomeStatement.xlsx	02i_Finance_LastFirst.pptx
02i_Newsletter.docx	02i_Finance_LastFirst.ppsx
02i_Outline.docx	02i_IncomeStatement_LastFirst.xlsx
02i_Shareholders.xlsx	02i_MergedLetter_LastFirst.docx
02i_Figure1.jpg	02i_Newsletter_LastFirst.docx
	02i_VaShareholders_LastFirst.xlsx

Capstone Exercises

You are the assistant director of the Information Technology department of Healthy Living Motorcycles, Inc. One of your responsibilities in this position is the maintenance of the company's database, which contains the Employees, Products, and Suppliers tables.

Create a Table and Import Data from an Excel Worksheet

You want to store the shareholders' information in the same database too, so you want to create a Shareholders table. Since you already have the shareholders' mailing information in an Excel workbook, you import the data into the Shareholders table. Then you add data to some of the fields, and then use the Input Mask Wizard.

a. Open the *02i_HealthyLiving.accdb* database and save it as **02i_HealthyLiving_LastFirst**.

b. Import the data from the *02i_Shareholders.xlsx* Excel file into a new table. Use the column headings from the Excel file, and let Access add the primary key. Save and name the table as **Shareholders**.

c. Ensure these field properties are as follows for the Shareholders table:

Field Name	Data Type	Field Size	Comments
ID	AutoNumber	Long Integer	• This is the primary key, and it is automatically created by Access. • Caption = Shareholder ID • Make sure that Indexed is set to Yes (No Duplicates)
S_FirstName	Short Text	30	Caption = S_First Name
S_LastName	Short Text	30	Caption = S_Last Name
S_StreetAddress	Short Text	30	Caption = S_Street Address
S_City	Short Text	35	
S_State	Short Text	2	
S_Zip	Short Text	25	
S_Phone	Short Text	20	

d. Use the Input Mask Wizard to create an input mask for Zip Code in the Shareholders table. Accept the underscore as the placeholder and store the data without the symbols in the mask.

e. Use the Input Mask Wizard to create an input mask for the Phone Number using the default Input Mask format for Phone Number. Accept the underscore as the placeholder and store the data without the symbols in the mask.

f. View the data in the Shareholders table in Datasheet view and adjust column widths so all data is visible.

g. Save and close the table.

Export Data to an Excel File

You want to write a letter to shareholders who reside in the state of Virginia. Before you write the letter, you create a query in Access to locate the Virginia shareholders, export the results of the query to an Excel file, and use the data file later when you write your letter.

a. Create a query in Access to find all shareholders living in Virginia, and name it **VA Shareholders**. Use all the fields in the Shareholders table except ID. Sort the results based on shareholder's last name.

b. Use the Export feature on the External Data tab on the Ribbon to export the VA Shareholders query to an Excel file.

c. Save the workbook and name it **02i_VaShareholders_LastFirst.xlsx**.

d. Do not save the export steps. Close Access.

Enter Formulas

Your executive assistant has collected enough financial data to create the income statement for the current year. You also want to project the income data for the next five years.

a. Open *02i_IncomeStatement.xlsx* in Excel and save it as **02i_IncomeStatement_LastFirst.xlsx**.

b. Enter the following formulas in the corresponding cells:
   - In **cell B8:** Gross profit = **Sales – Cost of goods sold**
   - In **cell B13:** Total operating expenses = **Selling expenses + Administrative expenses**
   - In **cell B17:** Income before taxes = **Operating income – Interest expense**
   - In **cell B20:** Net income after taxes = **Income before taxes – Income tax expense**
   - In **cell B23:** Earnings per share = **Net income after taxes / Total # of outstanding shares**

c. Copy the formulas from column B to the corresponding cells in columns C:G.

d. Use absolute references and the projected rates in A26:B33 to project the financial figures for Year 2019 in **ranges C6:C7**, **C11:C12**, **C15:C16**, **C18**, and **C22**.

e. Copy the cell contents in **ranges C6:C7**, **C11:C12**, **C15:C16**, **C18**, and **C22** to the corresponding cells and ranges in columns D:G. Delete any unnecessary cell entries.

f. Apply **bold** and add borders to cell B25. Format cells B26:B33 to display percentages to 1 decimal place.

Format Worksheet

To give the worksheet a professional look, you apply a document theme, merge cells to display the company and worksheet headings, widen columns, format headings, and apply cell styles. To keep track of the changes, you add your name and the date at the bottom of the worksheet. You also insert a footer to provide information on the worksheet. Finally, you preview and make necessary changes to ensure that the whole worksheet is displayed on one page.

a. Rename the first worksheet tab name to **Income Statement** and change the worksheet tab color to **Red**.

b. Apply the **Wisp Theme** to the entire worksheet.

c. Merge, center, and apply the **Heading 1 Cell Style** to the **range A1:G1** and increase the font size to **18**. Select the **Dark Red, Accent 1, Darker 50% font color**. Apply the **Dark Red, Accent 1, Lighter 40% fill color**.

d. Merge, center, and apply the **Heading 2 Cell Style** to the **range A2:G2** and increase the font size to **16**. Select the **Dark Red, Accent 1, Darker 25% font color**. Apply the **Dark Red, Accent 1, Lighter 80% fill color**.

e. Merge, center, and apply the **Heading 3 Cell Style** to the **range A3:G3** and increase the font size to **14**. Select the **Dark Red, Accent 1, Darker 50% font color**. Apply the **Dark Red, Accent 1, Lighter 60% fill color**. Move *Projected Income for the Next 5 Years* to the next line. Adjust all row heights as needed so that all headings are visibly displayed.

f. Apply **Heading 4 Cell Styles** to **range A6:A33**. Apply **Wrap Text** to **cell B25**.

g. Apply the **Total Cell Styles** to **ranges B8:G8** and **B20:G20**.

h. Format the following ranges:

   Range B6:G20 with Accounting Number Format and no decimal places.

   Range B22:G22 with Comma and no decimal places.

   Range B23:G23 with Accounting Number Format and 2 decimal places.

i. Adjust column widths to display all content in cells.

j. Use an appropriate date function in **cell A34** to display today's date in your worksheet. Use the **Short Date format**.

k. Create a footer with your first name and last name on the left side, the sheet name in the center, and file name on the right side of the worksheet.

l. Change orientation to **Landscape**, margins to **Narrow**, and bottom margin to **.5"**. Change the scale to 95%. Preview the worksheet to ensure that the whole worksheet fits on one page.

Create an Excel Chart

You create a 3D column chart for the projected Earnings per share (EPS) of the next five years.

a. Insert an apostrophe before the year in **cell B5** to format the years as text. Use the fill handle to copy the series to the **range C5:G5**. Ignore any error values in B5:G5. Apply **bold** and **center** the years in cell B5. Select the content in **ranges C5:G5** and **C23:G23** and insert a 3D Column chart that shows the projected EPS for the next five years.

b. Apply the **Style 3 Chart Style** to the chart.

c. Change the chart title to **Projected EPS for 2019-2023**. Increase the chart title font size to **28**. Add data labels with the Earnings per share above each bar.

d. Move the chart to a new chart sheet (following the Income Statement worksheet). Name the tab as **EPS Column Chart** and change the sheet tab color to **Yellow**.

e. Save and close the workbook.

Modify the Cover Letter and Newsletter

Your company periodically mails out newsletters to shareholders. Your assistant has written a draft of the cover letter and the current issue of the company's newsletter. You modify the letter and the educational newsletter to make them look more professional before sending them to shareholders later.

a. Open the *02i_Newsletter.docx* document and save it as **02i_Newsletter_LastFirst.docx**.

b. Convert the words *Healthy Living Motorcycles, Inc.* at the top of the document into WordArt. Use the **WordArt Fill: Red, Accent 4, Soft Bevel style**, and **28 font size**. Resize the placeholder so that the text displays on one line. Center the WordArt across the top of the letter.

c. Make the following changes to the letter:

   - Replace *Current Date* with a date field shows the month, day, and year and will update automatically.

- Insert **Educational information for Shareholders** after Re:
- Replace *Student First Name Last Name* below *Sincerely yours* at the bottom of the letter with your own name.
- Replace StudentFirst Name Last Name at Student@hl.com in the second paragraph with your own name and email address.

d. Format the whole document as follows:
   - Set margins to **Normal**, font type to **Times New Roman**, and paragraph alignment to **Justified**. Set the alignment of the References section to **Align Left**.
   - Select the text starting from *Educational Information* near the bottom of the first page to the end of the document, and set the paragraph Spacing After to **6 pt**.
   - Apply the **Organic theme** to the whole document.
   - Show All Markup and insert a **DRAFT** watermark as directed in the third comment.
   - Review all comments in the document and delete them.

Create Sections, Apply Styles, Modify Styles, and Change Bullet Image

The document describes several major topics of financial matters, and each topic is further broken into subtopics. You create a section to separate the cover letter from the newsletter, and format the titles and headings in each section using existing styles. You then modify the heading styles to enhance the appearance of the document.

a. Insert a **Section Break (Next Page)** to the left of the words *Educational Information* near the bottom of the first page. Apply the **Title style** to the section heading *Educational Information.* Modify the Title style to use **Times New Roman, bold, Green, Accent 1, Darker 25%, 6 pt** before and **12 pt** after. Apply **Align center**.

b. Apply the **Heading 1 style** to the following text in the document:
   - *Introduction*
   - *Understanding Financial Statements*
   - *Understanding Financial Ratios*
   - *Summary*
   - *References*

c. Apply **Heading 2** style to the following headings:
   - *Balance Sheet*
   - *Income Statement*
   - *Statement of Cash Flows*
   - *Liquidity Ratios*
   - *Leverage*
   - *Rates of Return*
   - *Stock Market Ratios*

d. Modify the Heading 1 style to use **Times New Roman, bold, Orange, Accent 5, Darker 25%**. Adjust the paragraph spacing to **6 pt** before and **6 pt** after, alignment to **Centered**, and Line spacing to **Single**.

e. Modify the Heading 2 style to use **Times New Roman, 14 pt, bold, Orange, Accent 5, Darker 25%**. Adjust the paragraph spacing to **0 pt** before and **6 pt** after, and Line spacing to **Single**.

f. Define new bullets by using Bing Image Search and the keyword *motorcycle*. Use the new motorcycle image as the bullet replacing all bullets found in the bullet lists in the document.

Insert a Worksheet from Excel

You want to show an example of an income statement in the newsletter. Because the income statement from the workbook is too large to show in portrait layout, you decide to insert two separate sections so that the income statement displays on a landscape layout.

a. Insert two Section Breaks (Next Page) on the blank line above the *Understanding Financial Ratios* heading.
b. Change the layout of the blank page to **Landscape**.
c. Open *02i_IncomeStatement_LastFirst.xlsx* using Excel. Select the **range A1:G23** from the Income Statement worksheet tab and copy and paste it to the page in the Newsletter that you just formatted to landscape layout.
d. Insert and center a figure caption below the table. Add the caption title as **Example of an Income Statement**. Change the font type and size to **Times New Roman, 11 pt**, and adjust the paragraph spacing Before and After to **6 pt**.

Insert Table of Contents

You create a table of contents for the newsletter so that readers can navigate to the specific topic more quickly. To conserve paper, you decide to insert the table of contents within the cover letter.

a. Position the insertion point on the blank line above *Sincerely yours* on the cover letter.
b. Click the **Table of Contents arrow** on the References tab and insert a Table of Contents with the **Automatic Table 1** format.
c. Change the font for the table of contents to **Times New Roman, 11 pt** and delete the word *Contents*. Delete the blank line above *Sincerely yours* so that the cover letter is on one page.
d. Save the document.

Insert a Footnote, Footer, and Hyperlinks

You insert a footnote on the first page of the newsletter to inform your reader that the sources are listed in the References section. You also insert the hyperlinks in the References section of the newsletter.

a. Insert the following footnote at the end of the first sentence in the Introduction section on page 2: **The materials in this newsletter are summarized from the sources listed in the References section of this document.**
b. Apply **Times New Roman, 11 pt** font to the footnote.
c. Position the insertion point on page 1, insert the **Integral style** footer, and check the **Different First Page** box. Format the page number to start at **0**. Change the font type and size of the footer to **Times New Roman, 11 pt**.
d. Go to the References section on the last page of the newsletter, format the six sources as bullets, and **insert hyperlinks** to the six URLs.

Complete a Mail Merge

You conduct a mail merge to prepare a mailing to the shareholders residing in Virginia by merging the newsletter you have prepared with a data source that you had created using Access.

a. Move to the beginning of the document. Begin a new mail merge, creating letters using the current document. The data source is the *02i_VaShareholders_LastFirst.xlsx* Excel file.

b. You want to send the letters to only two recipients, with the last names of **Jones** and **Williams**. Note: If you are not using the Wizard, click Edit Recipient list to select the desired recipients.

c. Replace *[Address Block]* with the <<Address block>> field. Replace *[first name]* in salutation with the <<S_FirstName>> field.

d. Merge all records, resulting in a seven-page document per each recipient, with the cover letter and the newsletter addressed to only two Virginian shareholders.

e. Save the new document as **02i_MergedLetter_LastFirst** and close all documents.

Create the PowerPoint Slide Show

You will use the EPS Column chart that you created as part of a presentation to the shareholders by the finance department. You begin by creating a blank presentation and importing an outline that your assistant created for you. You set up the title page, insert a header and footer, and then apply a design and color theme to the document.

a. Open a blank PowerPoint slide show and save it as **02i_Finance_LastFirst.pptx**.

b. Enter the following text into the placeholders on the title slide:

   Title placeholder: **Healthy Living Motorcycles, Inc.** Change the font size to **55**.

   Subtitle placeholder: **Presented By: Student First Name Last Name**.

c. Apply the **Retrospect** theme with the default variant.

d. Insert the *02i_Figure1.jpg*. Ensure the image is sized to the height of **1.5"** and the width of **2.22"**. Position it horizontally at **10.55"** from the top left corner and vertically at **0.19"** from the top left corner.

e. Use the **Gradient Fill – Tan, Accent 5, Reflection WordArt** to add the company's name **HLM, Inc.** Put it on the left side of the image. Ensure the WordArt is sized to the height of **1.01"** and the width of **3.1"**. Group the WordArt and image to create a logo.

f. Create a slide footer that displays the current date, the slide number, and your full name on each slide, except the title slide.

g. Create a handout header with your full name and a handout footer with your instructor's full name and the class. Include the page number and the current date to update automatically.

h. Create Slide 2 using the Title and Content layout, and add **Agenda** as the slide title.

i. Insert another slide using the Title Only layout and insert **Any Questions?** as the title. Drag the placeholder to the middle of the page and center the title.

Import an Outline, Format the Slides, and Insert a Chart

You import the Word outline into the current presentation between the *Agenda* and *Any Questions* slides. You proceed to format the other slides and make them attractive.

a. Select the Agenda slide and import the *02i_Outline.docx* file into the presentation.

b. Ensure the format of the slide footer, handout header, and handout footer that you had created for Slide 2 has been carried to the newly added slides (3–9).

c. Open the *02i_IncomeStatement_LastFirst.xlsx* Excel file. Select and copy the **range A1:G23** from the Income Statement worksheet tab, and paste it on the right side of Slide 3. Apply the **Medium Style 2 - Accent 2 Table Style**, an **Outside** border, and the **Brown, Accent 3, Lighter 40% Shading** option to the image. Increase the table height to **5"** and table width to **6.7"**.

d. Insert a new slide with the Title and Content layout after Slide 8. Copy and paste the EPS Column chart to Slide 9. Insert the slide title as **Comparison of EPS over Five Years**.

e. Ensure the chart is sized to a height of **4.4"** and position it in the middle of the slide. Delete the content placeholder.
f. Populate the Agenda page with the titles of all the slides.

Add Animation

Now that the presentation has been created, add animations to introduce elements at appropriate times and to create visual interest.

a. Apply the **Wipe transition** to the page on Slide 1 and add the **Emphasis - Pulse animation** to the company logo. Set the animation to start **After Previous**.
b. Apply the **Fly In animation to the bullets** on Slide 2 and set the timing to **After Previous**. Set the duration to **01.50** and delay of **00.50**.
c. Apply the **Shape animation** to the slide title on Slide 4, and set the timing to **After Previous** with a delay of **01.00** second. Apply the **Fly In animation** to the bullet list on this slide. Change the order so that the title appears after the bullets fly in.
d. Apply the **Font Color animation** to the bullet list on Slide 10. Ensure the timing is set to **After Previous**. Ensure the duration is set to **02.00** and delay of **00.50**. Apply the **Morph** transition to Slide 11.

Create a PowerPoint Show, Save and Close the Presentation

You want to distribute a copy of the presentation as a show for anyone who is unable to attend the presentation.

a. Run the slide show. Save the presentation.
b. Save the presentation as a PowerPoint Show (*.ppsx) and close the file.
c. Based on your instructor's directions, submit *the following:*

   02i_HealthyLiving_LastFirst.accdb
   02i_Finance_LastFirst.pptx
   02i_Finance_LastFirst.ppsx
   02i_IncomeStatement_LastFirst.xlsx
   02i_MergedLetter_LastFirst.docx
   02i_Newsletter_LastFirst.docx
   02i_VaShareholders_LastFirst.xlsx

Education Discipline

DISCIPLINE 3

Using Microsoft Office in Education

Rob/Fotolia

LEARNING OUTCOMES

- You will use Word to create several documents related to class orientation and parent communication.
- You will use Excel to develop a worksheet to assist with recording numeric grades and determining letter grades, and to summarize data related to a field trip budget.
- You will use Access to keep track of class resources and activities.
- You will use PowerPoint to create a presentation that serves as an orientation to class.
- You will work with an integrated project in which elements of all four Office applications are incorporated.

CASE STUDY | Working as a Teacher

An educational system includes many professionals serving at various levels of education. One can work in a private or public grade school, middle school, high school, trade school, college, or university. Within each level of education, there are a variety of positions, including administrators, such as superintendents, principals, deans, vice-presidents, and chief financial officers; support professionals, including curriculum specialists, librarians, school nurse, and technology specialists; and educators.

For this exercise, you will be assuming the role of a middle-school (8th-grade) teacher. As such, you prepare lessons, present material to students, enhance education with field trips and projects, calculate grades, maintain records as required by the school district, work with parents, staff, and other colleagues, and attend and present at conferences. For many of those tasks, you use Microsoft Office to develop documents, presentations, workbooks, and databases (Figure 3.1). Although an education professional is not required to be a Microsoft Office expert, it certainly helps to have a basic proficiency in Word, Excel, PowerPoint, and Access. For each of the activities presented in this exercise, you use one or more Office applications.

Education

Use Microsoft Word

Background

Educators are responsible for a multitude of clerical tasks that support the learning environment. For many of those tasks, Microsoft Word provides the ideal software solution. From the preparation of class newsletters and handouts to the development of all sorts of letters and memos, teachers make broad use of word processing in the classroom.

Skills:

Chapter 1

Adjust Line and Paragraph Spacing, Check Spelling and Grammar, Insert Headers and Footers, Select Paragraph Alignment, Use a Template

Chapter 2

Apply Font Attributes, Apply Styles, Create Bullets, Insert Objects, Insert Shapes, Insert WordArt, Use Borders and Shading, Use Indents and Tabs, Work with Sections

Chapter 3

Create and Edit a Table, Format a Table

Chapter 4

Create a Footnote

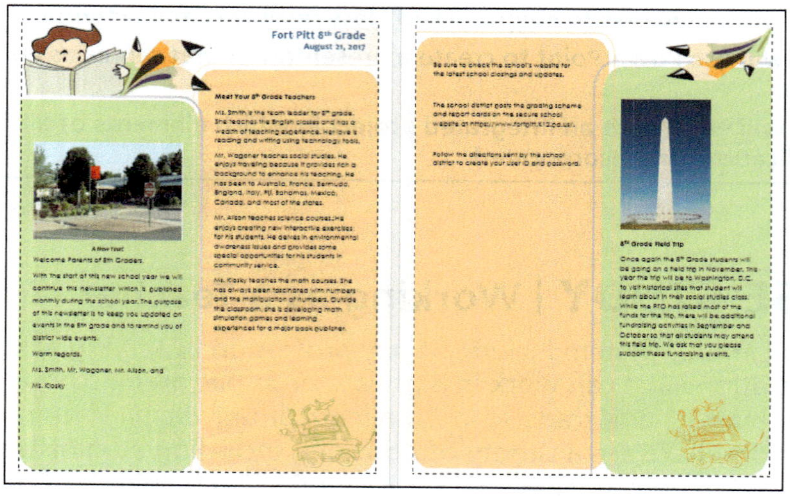

Word 2016, Windows 10, Microsoft Corporation

FIGURE 3.1 Working as a Teacher Document

CASE STUDY | Working as a Teacher

Starting Files	Files to be Submitted
03w_SchoolSupplies	03w_SchoolSupplies_LastFirst
03w_Rules	03w_Rules_LastFirst
03w_School.jpg	03w_Rules_LastFirst.pdf
03w_WashingtonMonument.jpg	03w_RulesPoster_LastFirst
03w_Class.jpg	03w_Newsletter_LastFirst
03w_NewsletterImport1	03w_LessonTemp_LastFirst.dotx
03w_NewsletterImport2	
03w_NewsletterImport3	
03w_NewsletterImport4	
03w_LessonImport	

Capstone Exercises

You are preparing for the start of the school year. This requires that you create several documents related to class orientation and parent communication. You develop a supplies list, a flyer and poster with classroom rules, a welcome newsletter for parents, and a sample lesson plan.

Create a New Document and Select a Style

The policy of the school district is to have students purchase their individual supplies. To assist with that, you create a list of supplies required for the school year. You open a document with a list of supplies, rename it, and then add and format a title. This document will list supplies required for 8th grade students.

a. Open *03w_SchoolSupplies* and save the file as **03w_SchoolSupplies_LastFirst**.
b. Type **School Supplies List** at the top of the page and press **Enter** twice.
c. Format *School Supplies List* as Title style. Center the title.

Add a Header, Adjust Line Spacing, Set Tabs, and Insert a Symbol

This school supply list was generated during a planning session with the other 8th-grade teachers, but each of you is responsible for adjusting the list for your students. You add a header with your name and grade level, adjust line spacing, insert a rectangular bullet in front of each item, adjust the indent and tab setting, and then add a signature line. The form will be signed by the parent or guardian and returned to you when all supplies are purchased.

a. Display the Ruler. Insert a Header choosing the Edit Header option.
b. Type your first name and last name at the left margin. Add a right tab at the 6" mark in the header area and remove the center tab.
c. Type **8th Grade** at the right tab mark. Close the Header.
d. Set the line spacing for the list of items to Double. Set Spacing After to **0 pt**.
e. Apply Bullets to the list of items to purchase. Define a new bullet, using symbol code **255** in the Symbol font group so that bullets display as empty rectangles. Students can then check off the items purchased so they can see what is left to buy.
f. Move to the end of the document and press **Enter** three times, inserting 2 blank lines.
g. Drag the left indent to **3"** on the horizontal ruler on the last blank line. Type **Parent or Guardian Signature**. Set a right tab at the **6"** mark. Press **Tab** and type **Date**.
h. Insert a line shape about 1/4" above the text just typed extending from the 3" mark to the 6" mark. Hold Shift while dragging the line to ensure a straight line. Change the shape style to **Subtle Line – Dark 1**.
i. Save the document and close it.

Modify a Document

You plan to review classroom rules and discuss them with your students. You also create a flyer for posting in the classroom.

a. Open *03w_Rules* and save it as **03w_Rules_LastFirst**.
b. Run the Spelling & Grammar checker. Make corrections as necessary.

c. Adjust the font size of all text in the list to **20 pt**. Change the first letter of the first rule (*Show respect for others*) to **28pt, Bold.** Use Format Painter to change the first letter of the remaining rules to **28pt, Bold.**

d. Change the color of every other first letter to **red**, beginning with the first rule.

e. Insert a Box page border using the **seventh style (the first double line)**, with a width of **1½ pt** and a Color of **Red**. The page border should be applied to the whole document.

f. Select all text and create a hanging indent at **0.25"**.

g. Place the insertion point at the blank line at the top of the document. Using the search keywords, *class raising hands*, insert an online picture.

h. Adjust the size of the image to **1.5"** in height. The width will adjust automatically. Set text wrapping around the image to **Top and Bottom**.

i. Insert a WordArt object, selecting **Fill: Red, Accent color 2; Outline: Red, Accent color 2**. Type **Classroom Rules** in the WordArt placeholder. Move the WordArt object to the right of the image, approximately centered vertically with the image, with the right edge near the 6" mark on the Ruler.

j. Ensure that the left side of the WordArt placeholder touches the right edge of the image. Apply Text Effect **Bevel, Round** to the WordArt object. Apply text fill of **Red**.

k. Save the document. Save the document again as a **PDF file** so the IT department can easily include it on the school website. Close the PDF file.

Change Formatting

You use the flyer you created to make a classroom poster. To do so, you adjust the paper and font size.

a. Click the **File tab**, click **Print**, and change the paper size to **Legal.** Return to Print Layout view.

b. Select all the text rules, beginning with *Show respect for others*, and change the font to **36 pt**. Select the first letter of each rule and change the font size to **48 pt**.

c. Adjust line spacing of the rules to **Single, 6 pt After**.

d. Adjust the font size of the WordArt to **48 pt**. Ensure that the WordArt text fits on one line, dragging the right side of the WordArt placeholder as necessary. Ensure that the left edge of the WordArt object touches the right edge of the image. Ensure that the WordArt object is approximately vertically centered beside the image.

e. Save the document as **03w_RulesPoster_LastFirst**. Close the document.

Use a Template

To create the first newsletter for this academic year, you use a template. You replace sample content with your own.

a. Create a new document using *newsletter* as the search term in the *Search for online templates* search box. Select the *Class newsletter* template and save the file as **03w_Newsletter_LastFirst**. If asked to agree to upgrade the file to a newer file format, click **OK**.

b. Click the **Date** placeholder at the top of the right column, click the **Date arrow** and select the third Monday in August of the current year. Click the **Weekly Class Newsletter** placeholder and type **Fort Pitt 8th Grade**. Bold the text you typed.

c. Insert the picture **03w_School.jpg** on the first page in the picture placeholder in the left column. Replace *[Photo Caption]* with **A New Year!**

d. Remove the content control, including *Dear Room 108 Families*. Remove any blank paragraph left on the line after the removal. Remove the next content control in the left column containing Latin text. Insert text from *03w_NewsletterImport1* in the left column. Insert a hard return before *Ms. Klosky* to ensure that the name is not broken between lines. Delete the extra paragraph mark at the bottom of the left column.

e. Remove the content control and all text from the right column on page 1. Ensure that all blank paragraphs are removed except the one that indicates the end of the column. Insert text from the file *03w_NewsletterImport2*. Delete the extra paragraph mark at the bottom of the right column.

f. Remove any content controls and all text from the left column on page 2. Insert text from *03w_NewsletterImport3*. Right-click the URL and remove the hyperlink.

g. Insert *03w_WashingtonMonument.jpg* in the picture placeholder on page 2. Adjust the picture height to **3"**. Right-click the **Photo Caption placeholder** on page 2 and remove the content control. Ensure that there is no blank paragraph below the picture on page 2.

h. Replace all text below the picture in the right column of page 2 with text from *03w_NewsletterImport4*. Change the view to Multiple Pages to see the complete newsletter layout.

i. Save and close the file, agreeing to update to the newest Word format if asked.

Create a Template, Use a Section Break, Adjust Page Orientation, Insert a Table, and Include a Footnote

Because a large part of your job requires creating lesson plans, you create a template to simplify that task. The template includes appropriate section breaks, attractive page orientation, and a table to summarize each lesson. You also include a footnote to identify the document.

a. Open the document *03w_LessonImport* and ensure that it is shown in 100% view. Save the document as a Word Template, with the file name **03w_LessonTemp_LastFirst.dotx**.

b. Place the insertion point at the end of the document and insert a page break. Change the page orientation to **Landscape** for page 2 only.

c. Insert a **5 × 3 table** at the top of page 2.

d. Type the following in the table. Text may not wrap exactly as shown here. As you type cell content, do not press Enter. Italicize all text in the second row.

Content Outline	Instructional Methods	Procedure	Materials	Evaluation/ Assessment
[Place the general outline of content here.]	*[What will the teacher do? What will the learner do? Examples include discussions, projects, lectures, demonstrations, and exercises.]*	*[Provide a step-by-step list of what will be done.]*	*[List materials needed; for example, computer with Internet connection, poster board, or notecards.]*	*[How will you assess learners' achievement of objectives?]*

e. Format row 1 with a **Box** border, using a **Double border style** so that it surrounds all four sides of the row. Shade row 1 with **White, Background 1, Darker 15%**.

f. Insert the following footnote after *Information Literacy* (before the closing bracket) in the Academic Standard line near the end of text on page 1. Include the period at the end of the footnote.

You may substitute the appropriate standard here. Example standards can be found at http://www.iste.org.

g. Save the template and exit Word. Based on your instructor's directions, submit the following:

   03w_SchoolSupplies_LastFirst

   03w_Rules_LastFirst

   03w_Rules_LastFirst.pdf

   03w_RulesPoster_LastFirst

   03w_Newsletter_LastFirst

   03w_LessonTemp_LastFirst.dotx

Education

Use Microsoft Excel

Background

Using Microsoft Excel, a teacher's task of organizing numbers and displaying results of calculations is simplified. Even when school districts provide online access for generating grade reports, many teachers prefer to first complete calculations in Excel. In fact, Excel streamlines a number of management tasks and statistical calculations that are necessary for meeting required standards. In addition, teachers deal with budgetary issues related to the classroom and other extracurricular activities—applications ideally suited for Excel.

Skills:

Chapter 1

Adjust Column Width, Apply Borders, Apply Number Formats, Copy and Paste Data, Create a Footer, Create Formulas, Format a Worksheet, Insert Rows, Insert Statistical Functions, Manage a Workbook And Worksheets, Recolor a Worksheet Tab, Rename a Worksheet, Set a Print Area, Use Autofill, Use Page Setup Options, Work with Ranges

Chapter 2

Use Relative and Absolute References, Use the COUNTIF Function, Use the IF Function, Use the SUM Function, Use the TODAY Function, Use the VLOOKUP Function

Chapter 3

Change Chart Color, Create a Chart, Create Sparklines, Format Chart Elements

Chapter 4

Create a Table, Filter Data, Sort Data

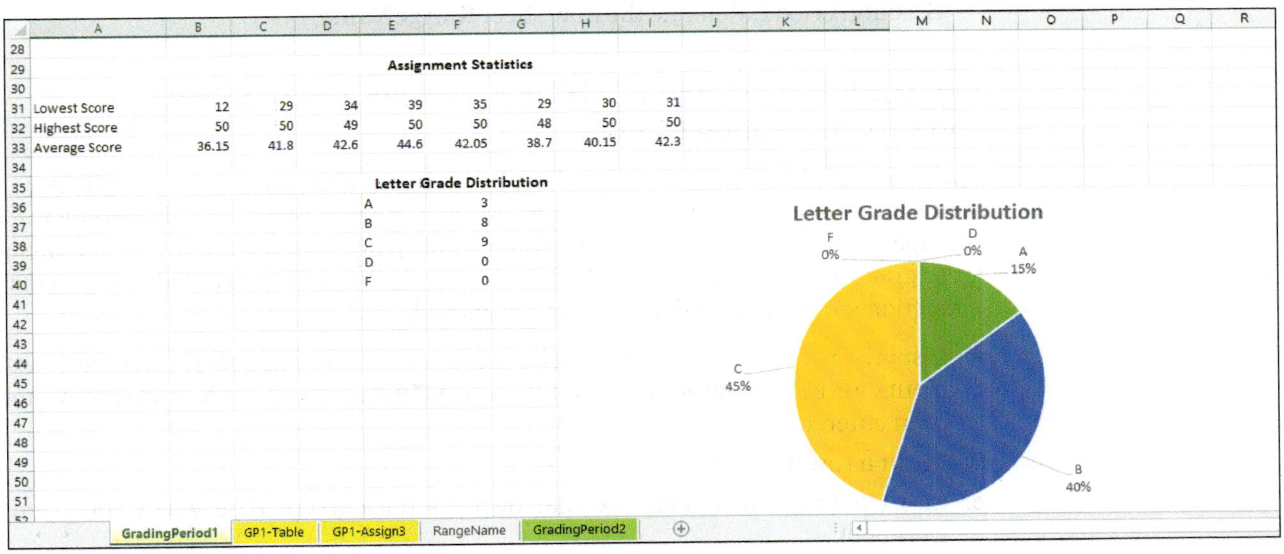

Excel 2016, Windows 10, Microsoft Corporation

FIGURE 3.2 Working as a Teacher Workbook

CASE STUDY | Working as a Teacher

Starting Files	File to be Submitted
03e_GradeBookImport	**03e_Grades_LastFirst**
03e_GradeBookImport2	

Capstone Exercises

Excel is an excellent tool for use in such classroom applications as calculating grades and maintaining budget records. You develop a worksheet to assist with recording numeric grades and determining letter grades. In addition, you use Excel to summarize data related to a field trip budget.

Create a New Workbook, Add Labels, and Rename a Worksheet

You create a new workbook, add labels, rename a worksheet, and save the workbook. The worksheet is designed to record and summarize individual student grades.

a. Open a new blank workbook and save it as **03e_Grades_LastFirst**.

b. Type **Academic Year 2017-2018** in **cell A1**.

c. Type your first name and last name in **cell A2**. In **cell A3**, type **8th Grade English/ Period 1**.

d. Type the following labels in the corresponding cells:

   B5 **Grading Period 1**

   A6 **Name**

   B6 **Assign1** and AutoFill this label through I6 so the last entry is *Assign8*.

   J6 **Total Points**

   K6 **Percentage**

   L6 **Letter Grade**

e. Rename *Sheet 1* to **GradingPeriod1**. Add a new worksheet following GradingPeriod1. Rename the new sheet **RangeName**.

Use SUM, TODAY, and LOOKUP Functions, Insert a Row, and Create a Range Name

You continue developing the worksheet by inserting a function to total individual student scores for the first grading period. Using another formula, you determine the percentage score for each student (based on possible points), and use a function to assign a letter grade for each student based on a table array. On a newly inserted row, you include a function so the current date is always displayed.

a. Display the GradingPeriod1 worksheet. Enter a function in **cell J7** that totals assignments for the first grading period (**range B7:I7**), even though grades have not yet been entered.

b. Insert a row between rows 4 and 5.

c. Insert a function in **cell A4** that displays the current date when you open the workbook.

d. Click in **cell G6** and type **Total Points Possible**. In **cell J6**, type **400**. Enter a formula in **cell K8** to calculate the percentage of total points possible that are represented by the value in **cell J6**. (Consider dividing total points by the total points possible.) Include an absolute reference where appropriate in the formula so the formula can be copied down correctly in the column later. Because assignment scores are not yet recorded, the percentage displays as 0.

e. Display the *RangeName* worksheet. In **cell A1**, type **Grades**. In the **rangeA2:B7**, enter the following data:

Percentage	**Letter Grade**
0%	F
60%	D
70%	C
80%	B
90%	A

f. Create a range named **Grades** for the **range A3:B7**.

g. Display the GradingPeriod1 worksheet and insert a VLOOKUP function in **cell L8** that will return a letter grade in cell L8 based on the percentage score from cell K8. The Lookup value is K8. You will use the Grades range located in the RangeName worksheet as the table array. The grade will come from the second column in the array.

Enter Data and Copy Formulas

To test the worksheet, you enter sample data and copy formulas. After correcting any formulas or functions, you delete sample data.

a. Copy formulas in the **range J8:L8** down to **range J9:L11**.

b. Click in **cell A8** and type **Student 1**. Use AutoFill to copy **cell A8** down through **cell A11**. In **cell B8,** type **50**. In **cell B9**, type **30**, and in **cell B10**, type **41**. In **cell B11**, type **38**. Use AutoFill to copy values in **range B8:B11** across to column **I.**

c. Copy the formulas in **cells J11** and **K11** down through row 27. Format the **range K8:K27** as **Percent Style**. Decrease the number of decimal places to **0**. Ensure that the percentage in column K is calculated correctly and that the correct letter grade is displayed in column L.

d. Copy **cell L11** down the column to **cell L27**. Having checked formulas, delete the data in **cells A8:I11**. Do not delete formulas or headings outside the range.

Format the Worksheet, Add and Sort Student Data, and Include a Footer

Having finalized student formulas and functions, you add student data, improve the appearance, and sort student records in alphabetical order.

a. Open *03e_GradeBookImport*. Copy cells A1:I20 from this workbook and paste them in the GradingPeriod1 worksheet of 03e_Grades_LastFirst, beginning in cell A8. Close 03e_GradeBookImport without saving. You do not need to save information on the Clipboard.

b. Select rows 1 through 7 and format contents as **Bold**. Change the font of the text in **cell A1** to **16 pt**.

c. Merge and center **ranges A1:L1**, **A2:L2**, and **A3:L3**. Apply the **Yellow** Fill Color to **range A6:L7**

d. Wrap text in **cell J7** and **cell L7**. Adjust the column width of columns A and K so that all contents are visible. Apply a border, selecting **All Borders,** around the range **A8:L27**. Right align the contents of **cell J7**.

e. Sort all student data in **cells A8:L27** by Name in ascending order (from A to Z).

f. Create a footer with your name in the center and the Sheet Name code on the right. Change worksheet orientation to Landscape.

Use Statistical Functions

The school district now requires that such statistical functions as highest score, lowest score, and average score be available for all student assignments. In addition, letter grades must be reported each grading period, so it is important to maintain those records.

a. Type **Assignment Statistics** in **cell A29** of the GradingPeriod1 sheet. Bold the text in **cell A29**, assign **12 pt font size**, and **merge and center** the **range A29:L29**.

b. Type **Lowest Score** in **cell A31**, **Highest Score** in **cell A32**, and **Average Score** in **cell A33**.

c. Enter a function in **cell B31** to calculate the lowest Assign1 score of all students. Enter a function in **cell B32** to calculate the highest Assign1 score of all students. Enter a function in **cell B33** to calculate the average Assign1 score of all students. Copy all three functions through Assign8 (column I).

d. Type **Letter Grade Distribution** in **cell A35**. **Bold**, and **merge and center** across **cells A35:L35**. Change the font size of the merged and centered cell to **12 pt**.

e. Type **A** in **cell E36**. Type **B** in **cell E37**. Type **C** in **cell E38**. Type **D** in **cell E39**. **Type F** in **cell E40**.

f. Include a COUNTIF function in cell F36 to count the number of As. The function should refer to the **range L8:L27** as an absolute reference and should refer to the grade in **cell E36**. Ensure that the reference to **cell E36** is relative, as it will be necessary for that cell to be adjusted as the function is copied down the column. AutoFill the function from **cell F36** to the **range F37:F40**, checking for Bs, Cs, Ds, and Fs, respectively.

g. Use the Page Setup dialog box to fit the worksheet to one page for printing purposes.

Copy a Worksheet and Delete Data

As the first grading period ends, you create a worksheet to record grades for the second.

a. Create a copy of the *GradingPeriod1* worksheet, locating the new worksheet as the last one and naming it **GradingPeriod2**. Delete all data in **range B8:I27** on the *GradingPeriod2* worksheet. The average scores on row 33 display an error message since there are no scores to average.

b. Change the Grading Period in **cell A3** to **Period 2**. Change the Grading Period in **cell B6** to **Period 2**. Change the fill color of **range A6:L7** to **Light Green**. Change the tab color of the GradingPeriod2 worksheet to **Light Green**. Change the GradingPeriod1 tab color to **Yellow**.

c. Open *03e_GradeBookImport2* and copy the data in **range B1:D20** into **range B8:D27** on the GradingPeriod2 worksheet. Because the second grading period is not yet complete, the final percentage score and letter grade does not reflect the actual student status. Close 03e_GradeBookImport2 without saving.

Insert Pie, Column, and Sparkline Charts

It is often easier to identify trends or current situations when worksheet data is charted. In this case, your principal asks for one or more descriptive charts diagramming data related to grades. You first create a pie chart of letter-grade distribution and then a column chart focusing on the third assignment. You also work with a sparkline chart to draw attention to a trend.

a. Select the *GradingPeriod1 worksheet.*

b. Create a **2D piechart** of the **range E36:F40**, showing the letter grade distribution for Grading Period 1. Drag the chart to position it between **cells H36** and **N50** on the GradingPeriod1 worksheet.

c. Create a chart title, **Letter Grade Distribution**. **Bold** the title. Change the font size of the title to **18 pt**.

d. Click **Chart Elements** beside the chart and modify data labels to display **Category Name**, **Percentage**, and **Leader Lines**. Ensure that the value does not show. Place the data labels on the **Outside End**. Drag the data labels away from the pie chart slightly so that a leader line connects each label. Ensure that no data label overlaps the chart title. Close the Format Data Label pane.

e. Click **Chart Elements** and ensure that the legend does not display. Ensure that the entire pie chart is selected, and change the color to **Colorful Palette 4** in the **Colorful** category.

f. Create a **3D Clustered Column chart** of Assignment 3 that includes the Assignment 3 scores for each student. Data for the chart should include both **range A7:A27** and **D7:D27**. Place this chart on its own worksheet and name the worksheet **GP1-Assign3**. Move **GP1-Assign3** between the GradingPeriod1 and RangeName worksheets. Change the worksheet tab color to **Yellow**.

g. Create a primary vertical axis title with the text **Raw Scores** and a primary horizontal axis title with the text **Students** on the 3D clustered column chart. Title the chart **Assignment 3 Results**. **Bold** the chart title.

h. Type **Grade Trend** in **cell M7** on the GradingPeriod1 worksheet. **Wrap text** in **cell M7** and change the font size to **12 pt**. In **cell M8**, insert a **Column Sparkline** that shows all assignment scores for Paul Abba. Copy the sparkline chart through **cell M27**.

i. Enlarge the pie chart on the GradingPeriod1 worksheet to span the **range H36:R53**.

Create a Table, Filter Data, and Set a Print Area

You are often asked to identify students who may qualify for school honors or scholarship possibilities. Similarly, you may need to identify students who struggle academically so they can be provided with tutoring or other assistance. Using Excel, you create a table so data can be filtered by certain criteria, thereby identifying various categories of students. In this case, you seek records of students who scored at least 45 on the first three assignments. Having filtered records accordingly, you identify print settings for future printing.

a. Copy the GradingPeriod1 worksheet to a new worksheet called **GP1-Table**. Move the GP1-Table worksheet between GradingPeriod1 and GP1-Assign3.

b. Create a table using **range A7:L27** in the GP1-Table worksheet. Filter the table to display students with a score of **45 or greater** on the first three assignments.

c. Set the print area to include column headings and data for the first three assignments of those students filtered in the previous step. Include columns A through D.

Include an IF Function

Each grading period, you identify those students who have earned a grade of A, acknowledging them with a note included in the grade worksheet. You develop an IF statement so that if a grade of A is shown, a note is recorded.

a. Select the GradingPeriod1 worksheet. Type **Note** in **cell N7**. Ensure that cell N7 is bold.

b. Create an IF statement in **cell N8** that places the text *Great job this grading period* in the cell for any student with a grade of A, leaving the cell blank (inserting a space) if the statement is false. The letter grade included in the Logical test box should be enclosed in quotation marks, as should the space in the Value_if_false box. Copy the function through **cell N27**.

c. Save and close the workbook. Based on your instructor's directions, submit 03e_Grades_LastFirst.

Education

Use Microsoft Access

Background

A typical teacher must maintain records for many purposes—from organizing student records and managing attendance to keeping an equipment and supplies inventory. Although much larger database applications, such as payroll, are maintained by a specialized staff, smaller classroom-related files are more often managed by individual instructors using such database software as Microsoft Access. Even if a school district does not support the use of Access, knowledge of database fundamentals learned from a study of Access can be transferred to other database software that may be required.

Skills:

Chapter 1

Create a Blank Database, Enter Data in a Table, Filter Data, Navigate Among Objects in an Access Database, Sort Data

Chapter 2

Create and Modify a Table, Create Lookup Fields and Use Input Masks, Import Data in a Table, Run a Query, Specify Query Criteria, Use the Relationships Window, Work with Multi-Table Queries, Work with Wildcards in a Criterion

Chapter 4

Create a Form, Create a Report, Modify a Report

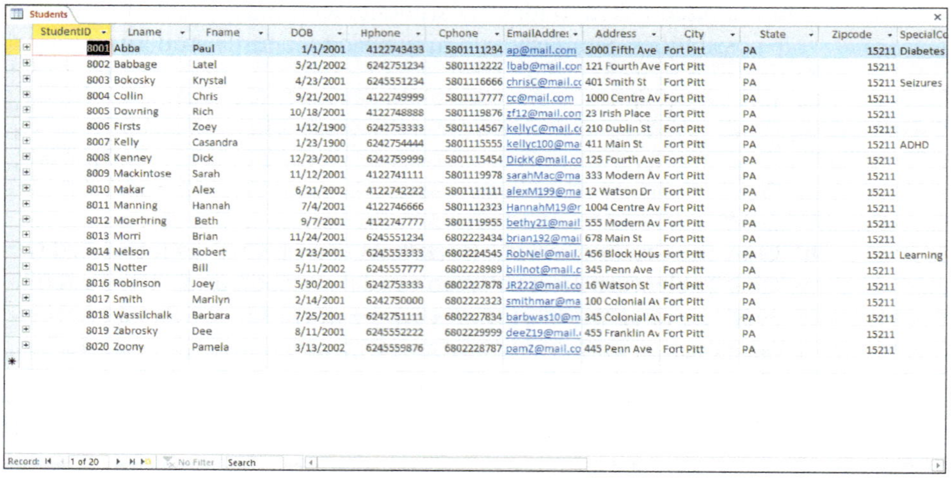

Students

StudentID	Lname	Fname	DOB	Hphone	Cphone	EmailAddre:	Address	City	State	Zipcode	SpecialC
8001	Abba	Paul	1/1/2001	4122743433	5801111234	ap@mail.com	5000 Fifth Ave	Fort Pitt	PA	15211	Diabetes
8002	Babbage	Latel	5/21/2002	6242751234	5801112222	lbab@mail.cor	121 Fourth Ave	Fort Pitt	PA	15211	
8003	Bokosky	Krystal	4/23/2001	6245551234	5801116666	chrisC@mail.cc	401 Smith St	Fort Pitt	PA	15211	Seizures
8004	Collin	Chris	9/21/2001	4122749999	5801117777	cc@mail.com	1000 Centre Av	Fort Pitt	PA	15211	
8005	Downing	Rich	10/18/2001	4122748888	5801119876	zf12@mail.con	23 Irish Place	Fort Pitt	PA	15211	
8006	Firsts	Zoey	1/12/1900	6242753333	5801114567	kellyC@mail.cc	210 Dublin St	Fort Pitt	PA	15211	
8007	Kelly	Casandra	1/23/1900	6242754444	5801115555	kellyc100@ma	411 Main St	Fort Pitt	PA	15211	ADHD
8008	Kenney	Dick	12/23/2001	6242759999	5801115454	DickK@mail.co	125 Fourth Ave	Fort Pitt	PA	15211	
8009	Mackintose	Sarah	11/12/2001	4122741111	5801119978	sarahMac@ma	333 Modern Av	Fort Pitt	PA	15211	
8010	Makar	Alex	6/21/2002	4122742222	5801111111	alexM199@ma	12 Watson Dr	Fort Pitt	PA	15211	
8011	Manning	Hannah	7/4/2001	4122746666	5801112323	HannahM19@r	1004 Centre Av	Fort Pitt	PA	15211	
8012	Moerhring	Beth	9/7/2001	4122747777	5801119955	bethy21@mail	555 Modern Av	Fort Pitt	PA	15211	
8013	Morri	Brian	11/24/2001	6245551234	6802223434	brian192@mai	678 Main St	Fort Pitt	PA	15211	
8014	Nelson	Robert	2/23/2001	6245553333	6802224545	RobNel@mail.	456 Block Hous	Fort Pitt	PA	15211	Learning
8015	Notter	Bill	5/11/2002	6245557777	6802228989	billnot@mail.c	345 Penn Ave	Fort Pitt	PA	15211	
8016	Robinson	Joey	5/30/2001	6242753333	6802227878	JR222@mail.co	16 Watson St	Fort Pitt	PA	15211	
8017	Smith	Marilyn	2/14/2001	6242750000	6802222323	smithmar@ma	100 Colonial Av	Fort Pitt	PA	15211	
8018	Wassilchalk	Barbara	7/25/2001	6242751111	6802227834	barbwas10@m	345 Colonial Av	Fort Pitt	PA	15211	
8019	Zabrosky	Dee	8/11/2001	6245552222	6802229999	deeZ19@mail.	455 Franklin Av	Fort Pitt	PA	15211	
8020	Zoony	Pamela	3/13/2002	6245559876	6802228787	pamZ@mail.co	445 Penn Ave	Fort Pitt	PA	15211	

Record: 1 of 20 No Filter Search

FIGURE 3.3 Working as a Teacher Database

CASE STUDY | Working as a Teacher

Starting Files	Files to be Submitted
03a_Books	03a_Books_LastFirst
03a_GuardianInput.xlsx	03a_Student_LastFirst
03a_StudentInput.xlsx	
03a_StudentGuardianInput.xlsx	
03a_AttendanceInput.xlsx	

Capstone Exercises

Maintaining educational records is a critical task for all schools and universities. As a collection of records, a database simplifies the organization of data related to such applications as payroll, accounts payable, and scheduling. On a much smaller basis, the typical classroom instructor must also maintain records associated with reordering supplies, managing grades, and organizing class projects. Although Information Technology professionals are responsible for district-wide record maintenance, individual instructors can use Access to keep track of class resources and activities. As an instructor, you maintain a contact list of students, parents, and information that would be helpful in an emergency or when you need to call on others. You also are responsible for recording class attendance for reporting purposes. Finally, you find a database helpful for organizing books required for a reading program. You know that Access makes it easy to enter data, create queries, and generate reports related to those tasks.

Create an Entry Form and Update and Sort a Table

Your school district has begun a reading program, providing selected lists of recommended books. Each student is to read two books from the list each semester, and an additional three books are required to be read over the summer. As you prepare for the fall semester, you review and update the Books database. Using Access, you create a form for data entry to simplify the task and enter a few new records.

a. Open *03a_Books* database and save it as **03a_Books_LastFirst**. If necessary, click Enable Content.

b. Use the Form Wizard to create a form based on the BookList table, enabling you to enter additional books. Place all fields in the form and use columnar layout. Name the form **BookList**.

c. Use the BookList form to add the following records. When all have been entered, close the form.

   Krakauer, Jon, Into The Wild, Anchor Books, 10, Medium, Fall

   Krakauer, Jon, Three Cups of Deceit: How Greg Mortenson, Humanitarian Hero, Lost His Way, Anchor Books, 10, Hard, Spring

   Krakauer, Jon, Where Men Win Glory: The Odyssey of Pat Tillman, Anchor Books, 10, Medium, Summer

   Guterson, David, Snow Falling on Cedars, Harcourt Books, 10, Medium, Spring

   Green, John, The Fault in Our Stars, Dutton Books, 10, Easy, Summer

d. Open and sort the BookList table by author last name in ascending order. Save the table.

Query a Database and Generate a Report

You query the BookList table to identify all books on a 10th-grade reading level. You will provide that list to some of the more advanced readers in your class.

a. Create a query, based on the BookList table, to display all 10th-grade level books. Include the LName, FName, Title, and GradeLevel fields in the query results.

b. Save the query as **10thGradeLevel**.

c. Use the Report Wizard to create a report based on the *10thGradeLevel* query. Fields shown include last name, first name, and book title. The GradeLevel field should not be displayed. Accept all defaults, but change the title of the report to **Books for Students at the 10th Grade Level.**

d. Change to Design view. Expand the report title placeholder to the left and right margins. Center and bold the report title text.

e. Shrink the last name field to the **1.5"** mark. Drag and resize the first name field to position it between **2"** and **3.5"** on the ruler. Resize the title field so the left edge is at **4"** and the right edge is at **8"**. Make these adjustments for both the Page Header and Detail sections of the report. View the report in Print Preview.

f. Save the report and close the database. You will submit the database when this project is complete.

Create a Database and Add Tables

Your job requires a great deal of paperwork in which you must report student attendance and participation. You also need to ensure quick access to each student's parent or guardian information. In both of those cases, an Access database in which you can develop specific tables of records will facilitate such record keeping. You begin by creating a blank database to house the necessary tables, reports, and queries related to attendance records. Student data that has been recorded in an Excel file will be imported into a new table. You also import two more Excel files, creating new tables related to students and guardians.

a. Create a *blank* database. Save the database as **03a_Student_LastFirst.**

b. Create a table named **Guardians**. Enter the following fields, data types, and field properties.

Field	**Data Type**	**Field Size**	***Properties***
GuardianID	Number	Field Size: Long Integer	Primary Key
PrimaryGuardian	Yes/No	Default Yes	Caption: Primary Guardian
GuardianFirst	Short Text	Field Size: 30	Caption: Guardian First Name
GuardianLast	Short Text	Field Size: 30	Caption: Guardian Last Name
EmailAddress	Hyperlink	N/A	Caption: Email Address
BPhone	Short Text	Input Mask: Phone Number with symbols in mask. Field Size: 14	Caption: Business Phone
CPhone	Short Text	Input Mask: Phone Number with symbols in mask. Field Size: 14	Caption: Cell Phone
Notes	Short Text	Field Size: 255	

c. Save the table and change to Data sheet view. Create a new record with a GuardianID of **5000**. Primary Guardian should remain checked. Use your own or fictional data for the remainder of the record, although the Notes field should be left blank. Save and close the table. Close any remaining open table.

d. Import *03a_GuardianInput.xlsx*, appending the imported data to the Guardians table. Do not save the import steps.

e. Open the Guardians table to confirm that new records were imported. Close the table.

f. Import *03a_StudentInput.xlsx*, creating a new table. During the import process, select the following settings:

- Do not allow duplicates for the StudentID field.
- Assign a primary key to StudentID.

- Name the table **Students**.
- Do not save the import steps.

g. Change the data type of the EmailAddress field in the Students table to Hyperlink. Close the table, saving changes.

h. Import *03a_StudentGuardianInput.xlsx*, creating a new table. During the import process, select the following settings:
   - Duplicates are not allowed for the GuardianID field.
   - GuardianID data type Long Integer.
   - GuardianID is the primary key.
   - Name the table **StudentGuardian**.
   - Do not save the import steps.

Create and Enforce Relationships

You build relationships between tables, linking them by common fields so that you can access data from several tables at the same time.

a. Add the **Students**, **Guardians**, and **StudentGuardian** tables to the Relationships window.

b. Create a relationship between the **StudentGuardian table** and the **Students table**, linking both by **StudentID**. Enforce referential integrity. The relationship is one-to-many.

c. Create a second relationship between the **Guardians** table and the **StudentGuardian** table linking both by **GuardianID**. Enforce referential integrity. The relationship is one-to-one.

d. Save and close the Relationships window.

Create a Multi-Table Query

You require a list of students with a documented health condition whose listed guardian is the primary guardian. For each student, you include several fields that identify the student, condition, and guardian.

a. Create a query to include data from **Students**, **Guardians**, and **StudentGuardian tables**.

b. Include the following fields from the *Students* table: **Lname**, **Fname**, **SpecialCondition**, and **Medication**. From the *Guardians* table include **GuardianLast**, **GuardianFirst**, **PrimaryGuardian**, and **CPhone** fields.

c. Show records in which the Special Condition field is not empty and the PrimaryGuardianfield contains a value of **Yes**.

d. Run the query.

e. Save the query as **StudentHealthIssues** and close the query.

Copy and Modify a Query

In preparation for an upcoming field trip, you list students who either have an allergy or are on medication so that you can be certain those students bring all required medications or make arrangements for any special health needs.

a. Make a copy of the *StudentHealthIssues* query, naming it **StudentAllergyMeds**.

b. Open the new query and remove **SpecialCondition** from the design grid. Add **Allergies** from the Students table. Move the Allergies field to the right of student's first name.

c. Show records in which either the Medications field or the Allergies field is not blank.
d. Run the query. Filter the **PrimaryGuardian** field so that only primary guardians are shown. Ten records are displayed.
e. Save and close the query.

Create the Attendance Table

The state requires accurate data related to student attendance. You create a table to simplify that task, including fields that identify students and attendance dates.

a. Create a new table named **Attendance** to include the following fields:

Field	Data Type	Properties
StudentID	Number	Field Size: Long Integer
AttendDate	Date/Time	
Attendance	**Use the Lookup Wizard to create a combo box with the following possible entries: Present, Absent Excused, Absent Unexcused.** Accept all defaults.	Field Size: 16

Remove the primary key from StudentID.

b. Create two records in the Attendance table as follows:

StudentID	8001	AttendDate	8/24/2018	Attendance	Present
StudentID	8002	AttendDate	8/24/2018	Attendance	Absent Excused

c. Save and close the table. Import *03a_AttendanceInput.xlsx*, appending the data to the Attendance table. Do not save the import steps.
d. Change the field size property of the StudentID field in the Attendance table to **Double**. Close the Attendance table, saving changes.
e. Open the Relationships window, add the Attendance table, ensuring that it is displayed to the right of the Students table, and then establish a relationship between the Students and Attendance tables based on **StudentID**. Do not enforce referential integrity. Save and close Relationships.

Create a Query Showing Student Absences

After a student has missed a certain number of days, a letter must be sent to the student's guardian. You create a query listing each occurrence of an absence for all students. The query is designed to show all absences, regardless of whether the absence is excused or unexcused.

a. Create a query to include data from the **Attendance** and **Students** tables.
b. Include the following fields: **StudentID**, **AttendDate**, and **Attendance** from the *Attendance* table, and **Lname** and **Fname** from the *Students* table.
c. Use the asterisk (*) wildcard to limit results to those records with the word *Absent* at the first of the Attendance field. In other words, the criteria should indicate that the word *Absent* begins the field, but any text can follow that particular word.
d. Run the query. Fifteen records should be displayed. Save the query as **MissedDays**. Close the query.

Create a Report Showing Total Missed Days

a. Use the Report Wizard to create a report based on the query *MissedDays*. Add **Lname, Fname**, and **AttendDate** fields to the report design. Accept all default settings, but ensure that the report title is **Total Missed Days**.

b. Change to Layout view. Select the Lname column header, hold down Ctrl, and click the top name in the last name column so that the entire column is selected. Drag the right edge of the column to the left to reduce the column width to approximately 2". Because a ruler is not shown in Layout view, visually approximate 2" in width. The exact measurement is not critical. Repeat the process for the Fname column, reducing its size to approximately 2 inches. Drag the Fname column to the left to better position it near the center of the page. Hold down Ctrl to select both the AttendDate column header and the first date shown, although the date most likely displays as pound signs. Drag the AttendDate column to the left to better position it on the page. Increase the width of the AttendDate column to approximately **2"**. Change the AttendDate column header to **Missed Days**. Change the Lname column header to **Last Name**, and the Fname column header to **First Name**.

c. Bold the report title and change the font size to **14 pt**.

d. Click the **Design tab** and choose the **Group & Sort** option in the Grouping & Totals group. Click **More** and click the **with no totals arrow**. Choose to show a subtotal in the group footer based on AttendDate.

e. Change the view to Print Preview. Save and close the report.

Use a Form to Update a Record

a. Create a form based on the Guardians table using the Form option. Save the form as **GuardiansInformation**.

b. Adjust the form as follows:

   Change the font size of the form header to **22 pt**, bold, centered.

   Change the title of the form to **Guardian Information Form**.

c. Save the form.

d. Click in the **Guardian Last Name box** and use the Search box on the status bar to navigate to Julie Makar's record, using her last name as the keyword.

e. Change to Form view and type the following in the Notes field: **Will be having surgery in October. The new contact is Nancy Makar, aunt, at 580-234-5610.**

f. Save and close the form. Check the Guardians table to ensure the update was made.

g. Close the table, save the database, and exit Access. Based on your instructor's directions, submit the following:

   03a_Student_LastFirst

   03a_Books_LastFirst

Education

Use Microsoft PowerPoint

Background

Microsoft PowerPoint is a widely recognized standard for presentation software. Many students are visual learners, and most are accustomed to the use of classroom presentations to assist in conveying and receiving information. The challenge for educators to create an energized and informative environment is simplified with the use of PowerPoint to support presentations.

Skills:

Chapter 1

Change Slide Layout, Create a Presentation, Create Speaker Notes, Format Slides, Insert a Footer, Insert a Table, Run a Slide Show, Use Animations and Transitions

Chapter 3

Arrange Objects, Create WordArt, Insert and Modify Shapes, Insert SmartArt, Insert Symbols, Modify Objects, Use Shape and Text Effects

Chapter 4

Insert a Picture, Insert an Online Picture

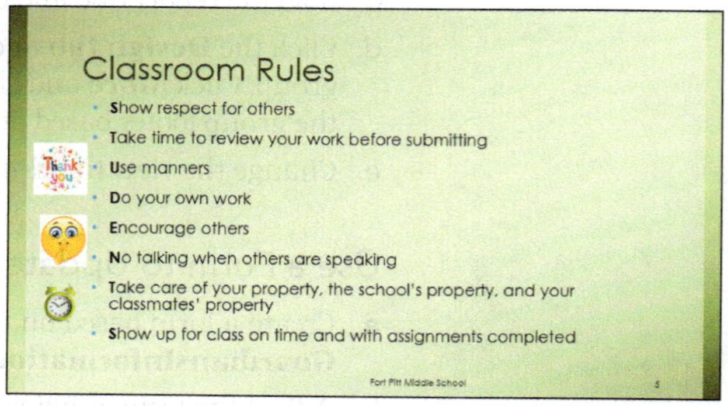

aliasching/Fotolia, Yael Weiss/Fotolia, Pavlo Kucherov/Fotolia; PowerPoint 2016, Windows 10, Microsoft Corporation

FIGURE 3.4 Working as a Teacher Presentation

CASE STUDY | Working as a Teacher

Starting Files	Files to be Submitted
03p_Rules.docx 03p_Agenda.jpg 03p_Principal.jpg 03p_Smith.jpg 03p_Alison.jpg 03p_Wagoner.jpg 03p_Klosky.jpg 03p_Computer.jpg 03p_Librarian.jpg 03p_Clock.jpg 03p_Talking.jpg 03p_Manners.jpg 03p_DCSkyline.jpg 03p_SpeakerNotesRules.docx	03p_OrientCR_LastFirst

Capstone Exercises

You continue preparing for the start of the school year. This requires you to create a PowerPoint presentation that serves as an orientation to class for your 8th-grade students and their parents. The presentation includes various slide layouts, pictures, SmartArt, WordArt, and a text box. Using transitions and animation, you add movement and energy to the presentation.

Create a New Presentation, Select a Layout, and Insert a Picture

The class orientation presentation contains critical information that you want all students to be able to view and revisit.

a. Open PowerPoint and create a new presentation based on a template. Use the keywords **Welcome back to school** in the *Search for online templates and themes* box, select the **Welcome back to school presentation template** and create it. Save the presentation as **03p_OrientCR_LastFirst**.

b. Replace *[Year]* on the Title slide with **2017–2018.**

c. Replace the current title on *Slide 2* with **Agenda** and the bulleted list with **Goals**, **Who's Who**, **Classroom Rules**, **Field Trips**, **Grading**, **Parent Conferences**, and **Questions.**

d. Change the Slide Layout of Slide 2 to **Two Content**. Click **Online Pictures** in the content placeholder on the right, and type **agenda** in the **Bing Image Search box**. Conduct a search and select the image of a clipboard with a pencil in the foreground. If the image is not available, select a similar picture. Change the picture height to **4.5"**. Drag the picture to position it approximately 1" from the right edge of the slide and vertically centered visually.

Insert SmartArt and a Text Box

Slide 3 presents bullet points related to a mission statement and/or goals. You add visual interest by customizing class information in the form of SmartArt.

a. Delete all text from Slide 3, with the exception of the word *Goals* in the title placeholder. Ensure that all bullets are removed but do not remove the placeholder. Change the font size of the title to **48 pt**. Click **Insert a SmartArt Graphic** in the content placeholder and select the **Step Up Process** graphic from the *Process group*. Type the following steps, creating additional steps where necessary. **Bold** step text.

   Read and follow directions

   Manage time: organize work

   Take notes: document sources

   Use appropriate technology for the task at hand

   Strengthen writing skills

   Complete work on time

b. Deselect the SmartArt graphic and insert a text box near the top right corner of the slide. Type **Success**, adjust the font size to **36**, bold the text, and change font color to **Dark Red**. Change the text box height box to **1"** and adjust the width to **2.5"**. Click the **Size dialog box launcher** on the Format tab. Expand the **Position** area in the Format Shape pane and indicate that the horizontal position of the text box is **10"** from the **Top Left Corner**. The vertical position is **1"** from the **Top Left Corner**. If necessary, drag the SmartArt graphic to better position it on the slide with relation to the text box. Close the Format Shape pane.

Insert Organizational Chart and Pictures

So that students will be introduced to the hierarchy of personnel with which they will work, you develop a slide containing an organization chart.

a. Delete all bulleted text and bullets in the content placeholder on Slide 4.

b. Insert a SmartArt graphic, selecting the **Circle Picture Hierarchy** diagram in the *Hierarchy* category.

c. Type **Principal in the top text placeholder**. Press **Enter**, and then type **Dr. Mangum**. Click the picture placeholder beside the text and insert *03p_Principal.jpg*.

d. Create the following as the second level under the Principal Level. Use the Text Pane to promote third level items to second level where necessary. Ensure that no third level placeholders remain.
   - Type **English**, press **Shift+Enter**, and type **Ms. Smith** on the second line. Insert *03p_Smith.jpg* in the picture placeholder.
   - Type **Science** in the next text placeholder, press **Shift+Enter**, and type **Mr. Alison**. Insert *03p_Alison.jpg* in the picture placeholder.
   - Type **Social Studies** in the next text placeholder, press **Shift+Enter**, and type **Mr. Wagoner**. Insert *03p_Wagoner.jpg* in the picture placeholder.
   - Type **Math** in the next text placeholder, press **Shift+Enter**, and type **Ms. Klosky**. Insert *03p_Klosky.jpg* in the picture placeholder.
   - Type **Computer Lab** in the next text placeholder, press **Shift+Enter**, and type **Mr. Ness**. Insert03p_*Computer.jpg* in the picture placeholder.
   - Type **Librarian** in the next text placeholder, press **Shift+Enter**, and type **Ms. Alendar**. Insert *03p_Librarian.jpg* in the picture placeholder.

e. Bold text in the text pane and change the font size to **12 pt**. Adjust the size and placement of text boxes in the SmartArt diagram so that a person's name is not divided between lines.

Copy Data from a Word Document and Insert an Online Picture

Earlier, you created a Word document containing rules of the classroom. You include those rules in the PowerPoint presentation, importing the document so there is no need to retype the content.

a. Replace the word *Policies* in the Title with **Rules** on Slide 5.

b. Delete all bulleted text and bullets in the placeholder and copy all test from the Word document *03p_Rules_LastFirst.docx*, pasting it into the placeholder area. Drag the bullet list slightly, aligning bullets under the *C* in *Classroom*.

c. Search for an online picture, using the keywords **on time** in the Bing Image Search box. Select an image appropriate for an 8th-grade classroom and insert it on Slide 5. Adjust the height to 1" and position the picture at the left of the *Show up for class on time* bullet. Following the same process, identify an online picture using the keywords **no talking**, resize the graphic to 1" in height, and position the picture at the left of the *No talking* bullet. Finally, identify an online picture using the keywords **thank you**, resize it to 1" in height, and position it at the left of the *Use manners* bullet. Use Figure 3.1 as a guide.

Change Slide Layout, Insert a Picture, and Create WordArt

This year, you plan a field trip to Washington D.C. The trip is a major class activity that will require plenty of planning and coordination. To build interest, you include a slide incorporating a picture from your computer files. Using WordArt, you add energy to the slide.

a. Change the layout of Slide 6 to **Picture with Caption**.

b. Insert *03p_DCSkyline.jpg* in the content placeholder.

c. Replace Special Projects in the placeholder below the picture with **Washington D.C. Trip**. **Center** the text.

d. Replace text in the bottom placeholder with **Participate in fundraisers to support our class trip to Washington D.C. in November.** (Include the period.)

e. Insert **WordArt** using **Fill: Green, Accent color 3, Sharp Bevel** style (second row, fifth column). Type **Class Field Trip**, rotate the object **Left 90°**, and drag the WordArt to the left side of the picture, aligning it attractively.

Insert a Table and Symbols

You use a typical 10-point grading system for all class projects and exams. The next slide communicates the grading system.

a. Remove all bulleted text and bullets in the content placeholder on Slide 7. Insert a **3 column, 7 row table**. Adjust the table height to **5.3"** and ensure that the width is **11.11"**.

b. Type the following in the first two columns:

Letter Grade	Percent Range
A	90-100
B	80-89
C	70-79
D	60-69
F	<60
I	Incomplete

c. Access the **Wingdings Symbol** set to insert four **smiley faces** (character code 74) in the third column of the "A" letter row, three **smiley faces** in the "B" letter row, two **smiley faces** in the "C" letter row, one **neutral face** (character code 75) in the "D" letter row, and one **frown face** (character code 76) in the "F" letter row.

d. Adjust the font size of the symbols in the third column to **32 pt** and change the color to **Dark Red**. **Center** the contents of the Letter Grade column, including the column heading.

Insert and Adjust a Shape, Insert WordArt, and Insert an Image

You are aware that a major factor in student success is parental involvement. You use a slide to encourage participation in parent/teacher conferences.

a. Delete the title placeholder on Slide 8.

b. Insert a **Wave** shape (from the Stars and Banners group) in the approximate position of the former title placeholder. The shape should be about 1.5" in height and should span the bulleted list below. Change the Shape Fill color to **Yellow** and apply the **Gradient, Linear Up** format from the Dark Variations category. Apply the shape effect **Bevel Angle**.

c. Insert WordArt, selecting **Fill - Green, Accent color 2, Outline: Green, Accent color 2** (first row, third column). Type **Parent Conference**. Change the text effect to **Wave Down** (a Transform effect). Drag the WordArt object on top of the yellow shape, visually centering it on the shape.

d. Replace items in the content placeholder as follows:
   - Conference Schedule
   - Sign-Up Sheet
   - Expectations
   - Contact via Email
e. Change line spacing of all text in the content placeholder to 2.0.
f. Remove bulleted text and the bullet in the content placeholder on Slide 9. Insert an online picture of a question mark. Resize the image attractively, approximately filling the space of the former content placeholder. Replace the title with the word **Questions**. Change the font color of the title to match the color of the question mark graphic.
g. Delete **Slide 10**.

Insert a Footer and Add Speaker Notes

For documentation, you include the school name on each slide and number slides. You include speaker notes to keep your comments organized and to make sure you remember to address all pertinent points.

a. Insert a footer with the text **Fort Pitt Middle School**. Include a slide number and make sure the footer is excluded from the title slide. Apply the footer to all other slides.
b. Select Slide 5. Display the Notes pane. Open the file *03p_SpeakerNotesRules.docx* and copy and paste all text from the document into the Notes pane. Change the font size of the notes to **12 pt**.
c. Type the following in the Notes pane on Slide 6:

   Encourage your parents to participate in the fundraisers to cover expenses for the field trip.

Use Animations

Animating various slide components adds movement and a level of energy to a slide presentation.

a. Select the content placeholder on Slide 5. Apply the **Float In** entrance animation.
b. Select the content placeholder on Slide 8. Apply the **Grow & Turn** entrance animation.
c. Apply the **Honeycomb** transition to all slides and ensure that the transition occurs upon a click.
d. Duplicate Slide 7. Change the font size of all symbols in the third column on the duplicated slide (Slide 8) to 44. Change the font color of all symbols to Green, Accent 3. With Slide 8 selected, change the transition to Morph. Preview the slide transition.
e. View the presentation as a slide show.
f. Save the presentation and close the file. Based on your instructor's directions, submit 03p_OrientCR_LastFirst.

Education

Integrate Microsoft Office Programs

Background

Microsoft Office applications enable you to integrate content from one Office program to another Office program. For example, teachers may use an outline from a Word document as a basis for a PowerPoint presentation. Teachers may import data from Access into an Excel spreadsheet or use a chart from Excel in a Word document. This ability to integrate and transfer content provides for timely completion of many of the tasks that teachers perform. In addition, teachers may use cloud services to collaborate on projects, to review and comment on files, and to back up files.

Skills:

Work with Mail Merge and Data Sources, Create an Excel Chart, Insert and Delete Comments, Use Styles, Embed and Link Content, Insert Comments, Create a Bibliography, Use OneDrive, Change PowerPoint Theme Color, Reuse Slides in a PowerPoint Presentation, Apply Table Styles in PowerPoint, Apply Font Attributes, Work with SmartArt

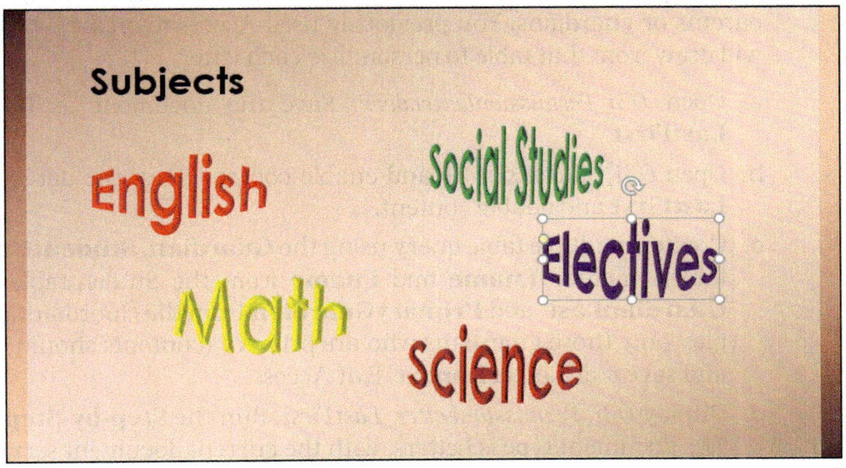

PowerPoint 2016, Windows 10, Microsoft Corporation

FIGURE 3.5 Working as a Teacher Presentation

CASE STUDY | Working as a Teacher

Starting Files	Files to be Submitted
03i_PermissionLetter.docx	03i_PermissionLetter_LastFirst.docx
03i_Students.accdb	03i_Students_LastFirst.accdb
03i_LessonPlanOriginal.docx	03i_LessonPlanOriginal_LastFirst.docx
03i_LessonPlanOriginal_MS.docx	03i_MergedPermissionLetter_LastFirst.docx
03i_OctoberNewsletter.docx	03i_OctoberNewsletter_LastFirst.docx
03i_ParentOpenHouse.pptx	03i_ParentOpenHouse_LastFirst.pptx
03i_POrientation.pptx	03i_LessonPlanFinal_LastFirst.docx
03i_ReadingBooks.jpg	

Capstone Exercises

The beginning of a school year is a busy time for educators. Each classroom has its own set of challenges related to keeping parents involved, preparing students for upcoming projects, and maintaining class records. The upcoming field trip to Washington D.C. is exciting for all, and you want to make sure parents are well informed as the time approaches. In another project, you and other teachers are preparing a standard lesson template that should simplify that job in the future. You are also excited about getting creative with a class newsletter. You know that Microsoft Office makes it easy to draw from its various parts so that you can create top-flight documents, presentations, and other files. For example, you plan to draw from an Access table of addresses as you prepare a letter to parents. For the newsletter project, a chart developed in Excel would be ideal for inclusion in the text. Learning to use Microsoft Office as a whole, drawing from its various parts as needed, is an important skill for educators.

Create a Primary Document in Word and Import a Data File from Access

So that parents will remain well informed on the class field trip, you send a letter to all parents or guardians. You previously used Access to create a table of addresses, so you will draw from that table to personalize each letter.

a. Open *03i_PermissionLetter.docx*. Save the document as **03i_PermissionLetter_LastFirst**.

b. Open *03i_Students.accdb* and enable content. Save the database as **03i_Students_LastFirst** and enable content.

c. Create a multiple table query using the **Guardian**, **StudentGuardian**, and **Student** tables. Include **Lname** and **Fname** from the Studenttable, and **GuardianFirst**, **GuardianLast**, and **PrimaryGuardian** from the Guardiantable. Add criteria to display only those guardians who are primary (contents should be **Yes**). Run the query and save it as **LetterImport**. Exit Access.

d. Display *03i_PermissionLetter_LastFirst*. Run the **Step-by-Step Mail Merge Wizard**. The document type is Letters, with the current document serving as the starting document. Recipients are located in an existing list, which is the LetterImport query in 03i_Students_LastFirst.accdb. You will not sort or filter recipients.

e. Place the insertion point after the word *Dear* on the first page of the Word document and insert a space. Insert **GuardianFirst** and **GuardianLast** fields, with names separated by a space. Include a comma after the guardian's last name.

f. Place the insertion point on the second page of the letter, in the first paragraph before the word *has*. Insert **Fname** and **Lname** fields (separated by a space). Ensure that a space follows the Lname field. On the same page, insert **Fname** and **Lname** fields (separated by a space) in the second body paragraph before the word *requires*. Ensure that a space follows the Lname field. The same two fields, separated by a space, should be inserted in the sentence beginning *I give my permission for*. Insert the names between the words *for* and *to*. Ensure that a space follows the Lname field.

g. Complete the merge, check the results, and then make any corrections necessary. Merge all letters. Save the merged document, which should include 40 pages, as **03i_MergedPermissionLetter_LastFirst**. Close the document. Save and close 03i_PermissionLetter_LastFirst.

Revise a Newsletter, Embed an Excel Chart, and Create a Bibliography

October is National Reading month, which is the school district's kickoff of a yearlong reading program. You create a bibliography reading list for the first half of the year for inclusion in the October school newsletter. In the same document, you embed a chart from Excel as an update for parents on the September fundraising event.

a. Open *03i_OctoberNewsletter.docx*. Save it as **03i_OctoberNewsletter_LastFirst**.

b. Place the insertion point on the blank row at the bottom of the *Happy Halloween* shaded area (table) on the first page. Insert an online picture, using the search keywords **row of pumpkins** in the Bing Image Search box. Select any row of pumpkins and insert the image. Adjust the height of the image to **1"**. Select **Center** alignment. The row of pumpkins should be centered, but not the remaining table text.

c. Save the document.

d. Open *03i_BudgetDC2017Updated.xlsx*. Save it as **03i_BudgetDC2017Updated_LastFirst**. Expand Column B to display the heading in **cell B8** on one line.

e. Create a **3-D Clustered Column** chart that shows for each resource category what was promised or raised and what was received. Do not include the total row in the chart. Move the chart to its own worksheet named **Funding**. Title the chart **D.C. Budget Update**.

f. Copy the chart and paste it into the first page of the newsletter, on the blank line below the text *Thanks to the parents who donated money to reach the goal of $1,500 to pay for the pool/pizza party!* Use **Paste Options**, **Keep Source Formatting & Embed Workbook**.Change the chart height to **2.5"** and adjust the width to **5"**. Ensure that the chart remains on the first page, adjusting chart size slightly, as needed.

g. Place the insertion point on the blank row below the text in *Important Announcements* on the first page. Insert an online picture of **books**, using Bing Image Search. Select any appropriate image. Change the picture height to **2"**. Delete the page break to ensure that the newsletter occupies only two pages.

h. Place the insertion point on the second page, under the heading *National Book Reading Month*. Type the following, pressing Enter after typing the paragraph:

   This month begins the first month of the school's book reading program to coincide with National Book Reading Month. The 8th-grade teachers and the librarian prepared this list for you to review as possibilities for your child. While it is acceptable to select any book you approve for your child to read, we will be providing additional suggestions in upcoming newsletters. Of course, the librarian can help your child select a book that will encourage an interest in reading.

i. Check spelling and grammar and correct any mistakes. Set the writing style to **APA**. On the blank line below the text just typed, insert a bibliography (without a title). Five books in the current source list will be shown.

j. Replace the picture on page 2 with *03i_ReadingBooks.jpg*. Rotate the picture to an upright position. Change the picture height to **1.5"**.

k. Place the insertion point on the blank paragraph at the bottom of the left column on page 2 (in the *More Important News* section) Press **Enter** and type **Washington, D.C. Field Trip**. Press **Enter**. Change the style to **No Spacing**. If an indent is inserted, remove it. Type the following:

   By now, you should have returned the field trip permission form. Without a signed form on record, your child will not be permitted to participate in the trip. If you have questions or have not yet returned the form, please contact Ms. Smith.

l. Change the style of **Washington D.C. Field Trip** to **Heading 2**. If an indent is inserted, remove it. Save and close the document.

Insert Comments and Share a Document

Teachers in the same school may find that they prepare lesson plans in a similar format—so much so that they might share a lesson plan template to simplify the task for all. You open a document prepared by another teacher that will serve as a template for many of your future lesson plans. By sharing the document online, you are certain that others to which you provide a link can easily access the document.

a. Open *03i_LessonPlanOriginal.docx* and save it as **03i_LessonPlanOriginal_LastFirst**.

b. Make the following comments in the document.

   Insert a comment for *[For example, Internet: Searching for Quality Information]* that reads **Should we place a note here to replace bracket information for each new lesson?**

   Insert a comment for *Objectives* that reads **Should we include a reference note here saying we use Bloom's Taxonomy?**

c. Save the document. Access your OneDrive account. Create a folder called **LessonPlan** and upload **03i_LessonPlanOriginal_LastFirst** to the *LessonPlan* folder in your OneDrive account. Close the document.

d. Share this file with your instructor, granting editing privileges, and providing a link.

e. Assume that your instructor has reviewed the document and shared it with you as *03i_LessonPlanOriginal_MS.docx*. Open the document from your data files. Delete the comments. Place the insertion point after the bracketed text on the first line, ending with *Searching for Quality Information*. Add a footnote with the text **Replace the text in brackets with the appropriate text based on the lesson plan topic.** (Include the period.) Save the document as **03i_LessonPlanFinal_LastFirst**. Close the document.

Develop an Open House PowerPoint Presentation

You prepare a PowerPoint presentation to assist in the open house held at the beginning of the semester. Parents who attend the open house will be informed of class activities and expectations. As you modify the presentation, you change the theme color and reuse slides from another orientation presentation.

a. Open *03i_ParentOpenHouse.pptx* and save it as **03i_ParentOpenHouse_LastFirst**.

b. Change the variant color of the current theme to **Orange Red**.

c. Change the color of the subtitle text on *Slide 1* to **Gray, Text 2, Darker 50%**.

d. Copy the English WordArt object on Slide 4 and paste it on the same slide. Drag the pasted object and change the text to **Math**. Similarly, copy and paste WordArt to create objects for **Science**, **Social Studies**, and **Electives**. Change the text fill of the WordArt objects as follows: Math = **Yellow**, Science = **Dark Red**, Social Studies = **Green**, and Electives = **Purple**. Arrange the WordArt objects on the slide, as shown in Figure 3.1.

e. Delete Slide 5. Replace it with Slide 7 from *03i_POrientation.pptx*. Change the table style to **Light Style 2 - Accent 2** in the Light section (second row, third column).

f. Delete Slide 6. Replace it with Slide 5 from *03i_ POrientation.pptx*. Delete Slide 7.

g. Change the font color of the title on Slide 7 to **Black, Text 1**, and bold the text. Delete all bulleted text, but do not remove the placeholder. Using the content placeholder, insert a SmartArt object, selecting **Vertical Bullet List** from the List category. Replace first-level bullets as follows, adding additional first-level bullets and removing second-level bullets:

   Reading program

   Lunchroom monitors

Fundraisers

Eliminate Hunger campaign

h. Delete the content placeholder on Slide 8.

i. Save and close the presentation. Based on your instructor's directions, submit the following:

03i_PermissionLetter_LastFirst.docx

03i_Students_LastFirst.accdb

03i_MergedPermissionLetter_LastFirst.docx

03i_OctoberNewsletter_LastFirst.docx

03i_BudgetDC2017Updated_LastFirst.xlsx

03i_LessonPlanOriginal_LastFirst.docx

03i_LessonPlanFinal_LastFirst.docx

03i_ParentOpenHouse_LastFirst.pptx

Science Discipline

DISCIPLINE 4

Using Office as a Science Professional

LEARNING OUTCOMES

- **You will use Word to write a formal lab report.**
- **You will use Excel to enter and format data, perform calculations, and create graphs and charts for lab experiments.**
- **You will use Access to organize, store, and analyze data and information collected from a scientific experiment.**
- **You will use PowerPoint to create a presentation to present the results of a scientific experiment.**

CASE STUDY | Working as a Science Professional

There are many different branches of science, including chemistry, biology, physics, earth and space sciences, environmental sciences, and the behavioral and social sciences. Given the technological advances in science and research, a career in science requires a certain level of expertise in computer competency, including a familiarity with a variety of software applications.

Strong organization skills are paramount for anyone working in science, especially while collecting and recording the results of experiments or compiling research for reports and papers. You also need to keep samples and research organized and accessible. In addition, the ability to analyze and draw conclusions from gathered data is essential. An Access database is an exceptional tool for organizing, storing, and manipulating data. Scientists also use Excel spreadsheets to compute and analyze data in tables, as well as to illustrate trends and make comparisons with charts and graphs.

In addition to organization skills, scientists are required to use word processing software such as Word to write reports and integrate data and graphs into these reports to communicate their findings or observations. Moreover, scientists may be required to use presentation software such as PowerPoint to convey the results of their studies to an audience.

Science Professionals

Use Microsoft Word

Background

College students majoring in the sciences are often required to write formal reports. Knowing how to create, format, review, and make changes to documents are necessary skills. It is important that students understand the features of Microsoft Word that are available in order to create an effective scientific document.

Skills:

Chapter 1

Review Spelling and Grammar, Insert Page Number, Insert a Symbol, Adjust Margins, View a Document and Manage Page Flow, Customize Document Properties, Insert Text and Navigate a Document, Use Smart Lookup and the Thesaurus

Chapter 2

Apply Font Attributes; Modify Styles; Change Paragraph Alignment; Change Line and Paragraph Spacing; Create a Bulleted List; Insert a Textbox; Modify, Move and Resize a Textbox; Format Text into Columns

Chapter 3

Create or Draw a Table, Insert Rows and Columns, Merge Cells, Change Row Height and Column Width, Adjust Table Position and Alignment, Format Table Text, Use a Formula, Convert Text to a Table, Create a Footnote

Chapter 4

View and Reply to Comments, Use Track Changes, Accept and Reject Changes, Create a Source

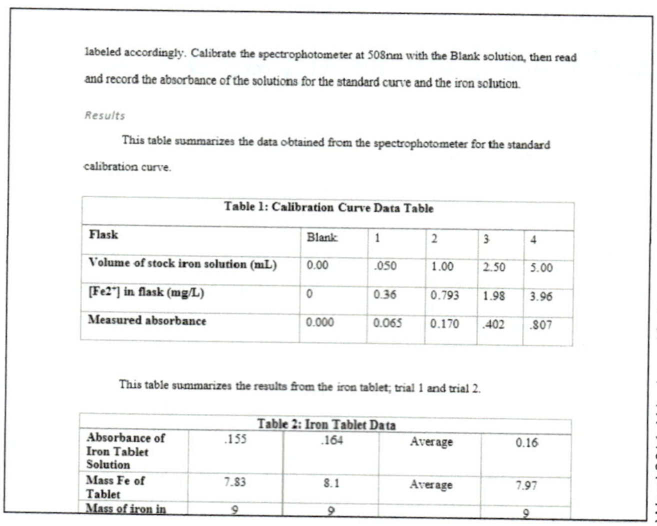
labeled accordingly. Calibrate the spectrophotometer at 508nm with the Blank solution, then read and record the absorbance of the solutions for the standard curve and the iron solution.

Results

This table summarizes the data obtained from the spectrophotometer for the standard calibration curve.

Table 1: Calibration Curve Data Table

Flask	Blank	1	2	3	4
Volume of stock iron solution (mL)	0.00	.050	1.00	2.50	5.00
$[Fe2^{+}]$ in flask (mg/L)	0	0.36	0.793	1.98	3.96
Measured absorbance	0.000	0.065	0.170	.402	.807

This table summarizes the results from the iron tablet; trial 1 and trial 2.

Table 2: Iron Tablet Data

Absorbance of Iron Tablet Solution	.155	.164	Average	0.16
Mass Fe of Tablet	7.83	8.1	Average	7.97
Mass of iron in	9	9		9

Word 2016, Windows 10, Microsoft Corporation

FIGURE 4.1 Working as a Science Professional Document

CASE STUDY | Working as a Science Professional

Starting Files	Files to be Submitted
04w_Report **04w_Conclusion**	**04w_Report_LastFirst**

Capstone Exercises

You are a student taking an introductory chemistry course. You are required to write a formal, typed laboratory report in conjunction with the experiment you and your lab partner just completed. You wrote up the preliminary report and asked your partner to review it and make corrections or additions. You now need to add the data tables and format it according to the instructor's specifications before you submit it to the professor.

Track Revisions

Your lab partner has reviewed the initial lab report, and has made some changes and inserted some comments. You need to review the document comments and accept or reject the revisions before you add additional content.

a. Open *04w_Report.docx* and save it as **04w_Report_LastFirst**.

b. Ensure that the markup view is All Markup on the Review tab, in the Tracking group. With the insertion point at the top of the page, use Next Change in the Changes group to move to the last sentence in paragraph one of the Procedure section that has to do with the accuracy of this experiment ("*If you are not careful . . .*"). Reject the insertion of this sentence.

c. Accept the insertion of the sentence in the next paragraph that begins with ("*Let the solution cool . . .*").

d. Reply to the comment by typing, **I will add the conclusions we mentioned yesterday.**

e. Turn off the Tracking feature on the Review tab, change the markup view to No Markup, and then move to the beginning of the document.

Format the Document

The instructor has distributed the formatting specifications. Apply the following formatting features to meet the requirements for the paper.

a. Add your name after *Name:*, your instructor's name after *Lab Partner*, and insert current date after *Date:*.

b. Set the left and right margins to **1"**.

c. Insert a page number at the bottom of the page using **Bold Numbers 3**.

d. Select the entire document and change the font to **Times New Roman**, font size **12 pt**.

e. Center align the title of the document and change the font size to **14 pt**.

f. Right align the information above the title of the paper beginning with *Name:* and ending with *Date:*. Change the line spacing to single.

g. Apply the **Subtitle** style to all of the headings (*Abstract, Introduction, Materials, Procedure, Results, Conclusion,* and *References*).

h. Modify the Subtitle style to font size **12 pt** and **Italic** and then update the Subtitle style.

Format the *Materials* Section

The list in the *Materials* section needs to be formatted as a bulleted list and needs a text box added to include an equation and the name of the equation to be used. There are many built-in equations in Word, and many more available from Office.com, but not many for use in chemistry. You can use the Insert New Equation feature to write your own equation, which is an ink-to-math feature where you can write out equations with your stylus, finger, or mouse, and have Word convert them to text.

a. Select the list of materials and convert it to a bulleted list.

b. Format the list to two columns.

c. Draw a text box just below the list of materials and type **Dilution Equation ($M_1V_1 = M_2V_2$)**. Apply subscript to the numbers in the equation.

d. Format the text in the text box to Times New Roman, font size **12 pt**, No Outline, and change the height of the textbox to **0.3″** and the width to **2.5″**.

e. Change the text wrapping to Square and center align the textbox.

Create a New Table

You need to add a table to the *Procedure* section of the report.

a. Insert a blank line after the first paragraph in the *Procedure* section.

b. Create a table with five columns and six rows.

c. Merge the cells of the first row and type the following: **Preparation of Standards Solutions.**

d. Enter the following headings and data:

Solution	mL Stock Iron Solution	Drops of Citrate	mL Hydroquinone	mL Phenanthroline
1	1	6	1	1.5
2	2	12	1	1.5
3	3	18	1	1.5
4	5	30	1	1.5

e. Insert a row below the headings, type **Blank** as the *Solution* type, and then complete the rest of the row with the following data:

Blank	0	0	0	1.5

f. Change the line spacing of row 2 to Single with no spacing after.

g. Change the height of row 2 to **0.4**.

h. Format the table using the **Grid Table 1 Light** table style.

i. Center align the contents of the table cells.

j. Add a footnote to the *mL Stock Iron Solution* heading: **Stock iron solution provided by instructor.**

Use Advanced Table Features

Some of the data from the experiment was entered into a table in the Results section and some of the data was not. It needs to be improved and some calculations need to be performed, using the Formula feature found on the Table Tools Layout tab.

a. Insert a new row above the first row in the first table in the Results section, to add a title. Type **Table 1: Calibration Curve Data Table.**

b. Merge the cells and top center align the title.

c. Format the table to AutoFit Window and apply the **Grid Table 1 Light** table style.

d. Select the four paragraphs of text below the paragraph *This table summarizes the results* and convert the text to a table with four columns.

e. Insert a new column on the right. Create a formula to average the two trial amounts for the Absorbance of the Iron Tablet Solution, the Mass of the Fe of Tablet, the Mass of Iron in Tablet, and the Percent Error.

f. Insert a new row above the first row in the table to add a title. Type **Table 2: Iron Tablet Data**, merge the cells, and then center align the title.
g. Center align the contents of Table 2.
h. Format the table using the **Grid Table 1 Light** table style.

Create a Source and Add It to the Document

The instructor created this experiment based on a journal article. You need to create the source, add it to the Reference section, and format it accordingly.

a. Using Manage Sources on the References tab, add a new source using the APA style for a journal article:

   Author: **Atkins, Robert C.**

   Title: **Colorimetric Determination of Iron in Vitamin Supplement Tablets: A General Chemistry Experiment**

   Journal Name: **Journal of Chemical Education**

   Year: **1975**

   Page: **550**

b. Click on the blank line below the References section. Select **Insert Bibliography** to insert the source.

Final Review of the Document

As you proofread the report, you realize you need to make a few more additions and changes to the document. For additional support on how to do something, use the Tell Me feature.

a. Insert missing text in the third paragraph of the Introduction section. As you begin to review the report, you notice that the formula for Beer's Law is incomplete: *Beer's Law* $(A = bc)$. Insert the symbol ε (Greek Small Letter Epsilon: 03B5, which can be found in Font: Times New Roman Subset: Greek and Coptic), so that the formula reads $A = \varepsilon bc$.
b. Add a few sentences to the conclusion section. Type the following under the Conclusion heading:

   The vitamin tablet was tested twice, and the results were in an acceptable percent error range. Miscalculations in this experiment can be traced to the difficulties in measuring the volume in the graduated cylinder and Erlenmeyer flasks. With experience, technical variations may be overcome. Overall, the vitamin tablet tested did come close to the amounts claimed by the manufacturer.

c. Insert text from 04w_Conclusion as new paragraph after the paragraph that you just typed.
d. Perform a Spelling & Grammar check of the document. Accept all references to *analyte* as the correct spelling, and accept *HCl, pipet,* and *phenanthroline* as correct.
e. Select the word *analyzed* in the second sentence of the Abstract section. Use Smart Lookup, in the Insights Group to review the definition.
f. Use the Thesaurus to replace *analyzed* with **evaluated.**
g. Insert a page break before the Conclusion section.

Change the Document Properties and Save the Document

a. Add the keywords: **Iron, Beer's Law, Absorbance** to the Advanced Properties dialog box.
b. Save and close the document.
c. Based on your instructor's directions, submit the following:

   04w_Report_LastFirst

Science Professionals

Use Microsoft Excel

Background

College students taking science courses often perform experiments to test a hypothesis. Data is recorded in a lab notebook. Knowing how to use Microsoft Excel to enter and format data, perform calculations, and create charts is required. It is important that students are proficient in using Microsoft Excel.

Skills:

Chapter 1

Adjust Column Width, Apply Alignment and Font Options, Apply Number Formats, Copy Formulas, Enter Formulas, Enter Text, Enter Values, Merge and Center Labels, Rename a Worksheet, Select a Range

Chapter 2

Create a Lookup Table, Determine Results with the IF Function, Insert Statistical Functions, Use Cell References in Formulas, Use the Average Function, Use the VLOOKUP Function

Chapter 3

Add and Format Axis Titles, Add Chart Elements, Apply a Chart Style, Create a Line Chart, Create an XY (Scatter) Chart, Format Axes, Format Chart Elements, Move a Chart, Position the Legend

Chapter 4

Add and Delete Fields, Apply a Table Style, Apply Conditional Formatting, Create a Table, Create Conditional Formatting Rule, Select Page Setup Options, Sort Multiple Fields, Use Structured References

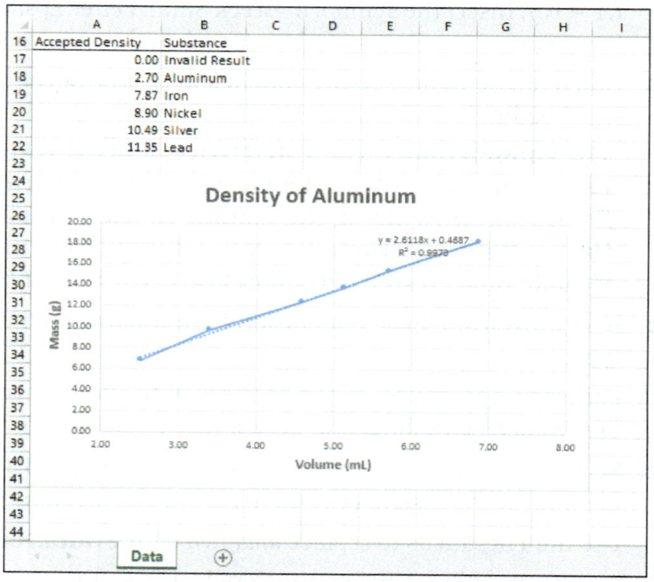

Excel 2016, Windows 10, Microsoft Corporation

FIGURE 4.2 Working as a Science Professional Worksheet

CASE STUDY | Working as a Science Professional

Starting Files	Files to be Submitted
04e_FermentationLab	**04e_FermentationLab_LastFirst** **04e_DensityLab_LastFirst**

Capstone Exercises

You have a busy semester with your science classes, and all of them expect you to be able to use Excel to report your findings, perform calculations, and create visual representations of the data. You recorded the results of your chemistry experiment in your lab notebook, and now it is time to enter the data into Excel. When you finish entering the data, you will create formulas and generate some charts. For your biology course, you conducted an experiment and created an Excel workbook to record your results. You want to use the table feature to filter and sort the data to analyze the results. You also need to create a chart to visualize one of the categories of your experiment.

Enter and Format the Text Labels

You are ready to create the first Excel worksheet. You have planned the structure of your worksheet and decide to enter all of the labels first and do some basic formatting before you enter the values and create formulas. You make sure that you have placed the data—in this case, volume before mass—to make the creation of charts easier.

a. Create a new workbook and save it as **04e_DensityLab_LastFirst**.
b. Type the worksheet title, **Density Determination of Unknown Metal Sample**, in **cell A1**.
c. Merge and center the **range A1:G1**. Middle Align the merged cell.
d. Apply bold and 16 pt font.
e. Select **row 1** and format the row height to **35**.
f. Rename the sheet **Data**.
g. Type the following labels:
   - **Sample ID** in **cell A3**
   - **Volume (mL)** in **cell B3**
   - **Mass (g)** in **cell C3**
   - **Density (g/mL)** in **cell D3**
   - **Average Density** in **cell A12**
   - **Standard Deviation** in **cell A13**
   - **Identity of Sample** in **cell A14**
h. Wrap the text in the **range A3:D3**; apply bold; change the fill color to **Blue, Accent 1, Lighter 60%;** and center align the contents.
i. Select column A and format it using AutoFit Column Width.

Enter the Lab Data

Using the data recorded in your lab notebook, you are ready to enter your results. You were given six metal samples of varying mass, and using the volume displacement method, you need to determine what kind of metal the sample is. You have already calculated the volume of each sample (subtracting the initial water volume from the final water volume).

a. Enter the data into your Data worksheet as shown below:

	A	B	C	D	E	F	G
1	**Density Determination of Unknown Metal Sample**						
2							
3	**Sample ID**	**Volume (mL)**	**Mass (g)**	**Density (g/mL)**			
4	1	2.51	6.75				
5	2	3.39	9.70				
6	3	4.59	12.44				
7	4	5.13	13.80				
8	5	5.72	15.44				
9	6	6.87	18.36				
10							

b. Format the **range B4:C9** with the Number format, with two decimals.

c. Select the **range A4:A9** and center the Sample IDs.

Use Formulas and Functions

Now that you have designed your worksheet and entered the data, you are ready to create a formula to determine the density of each sample. You also need to calculate the average density and standard deviation.

a. Create a formula in **cell D4**, to determine the density of each sample. Density = Mass/Volume.

b. Copy the formula for the rest of the samples.

c. Enter a function in **cell C12** to calculate the average density of all the samples.

d. Create a formula in **cell C13** to calculate the standard deviation (STDEVA) for the **range D4:D9**.

e. Format the **ranges D4:D9** and **C12:C13** with the Number format with two decimal places.

Use a Lookup Function

You also need to make sure your worksheet contains information for the true density (accepted density) of known metal substances so you can identify your sample. You will enter the density of known substances in your worksheet, and then use a lookup function to assign the substance name that corresponds with the average density result.

a. Create a lookup table starting in **cell A16**, using the data shown below. Apply the **Number** format, with two decimals to the values. Add a bottom border to the **range A16:B16**.

Accepted Density	**Substance**
11.35	Lead
7.87	Iron
10.49	Silver
2.70	Aluminum
8.90	Nickel
0	Invalid Result

b. Select column B and change the column width to **12.75.**

c. Select the **range A17:B22** and sort the table **Smallest to Largest on column A**.

d. Create a VLOOKUP function in **cell C14** that returns the name of the substance based on the average density.

Create the X,Y (Scatter) Chart

A useful way to view and present the data is with a chart, which provides a visual summary of the experiment. Use caution if you create a chart using Quick Analysis. In Excel, the scatter chart is the only graph where the *x*-axis is treated as a numerical value. You will need to show the linear relationship for the densities of each sample and add a trendline to show *linear regression* (a line of best fit through the data).

a. Select the values only for the volume and mass of each sample (**range B4:C9**), and create a scatter chart.

b. Move the chart below the lookup table and resize to span the **range A24:H41**.

c. Select the Chart Title placeholder and type **Density of Aluminum**. Apply bold and 20 pt font to the title.

d. Add axis titles: **Volume (mL)** to the primary horizontal axis and **Mass (g)** to the primary vertical axis. Apply bold and 12 pt font to the labels.

e. Format the horizontal axis so that the minimum bound is 2.0 because all volumes start after this point.

f. Add a linear trendline and choose the options to Display Equation and Display *R*-squared Value on chart.

g. Save and close the workbook.

Create and Format a Table

Your biology experiment on yeast fermentation under a variety of conditions has been completed. You have created a worksheet for the all of the fermentation data and one for just the results of one of the substances. You want to work with the data using Excel's table features but also may need to work with your original worksheet, so you decide to copy the worksheet first and convert the data to a table.

a. Open the *04e_FermentationLab* workbook and save it as **04e_FermentationLab_LastFirst**.

b. Select the **Fermentation Data** worksheet and copy it to a new worksheet. Rename the duplicate worksheet **Fermentation Data Table**. Change the tab color of the new sheet to **Blue**. Move the Fermentation Data Sheet Table worksheet to the right of the Fermentation Data worksheet.

c. Click any cell within the data **range A4:P25** and convert the data to a table.

d. Apply the **Table Style Medium 6** table style.

e. Delete Column C in the table, because 0 minutes is not needed for the analysis.

f. Merge and center the title over the **range A1:P1**, change the font size to 16 pt, and then apply **Blue, Accent 5 fill color**.

Filter and Sort the Table Data and Use a Structured Reference

As you look over your results, you would like to try to analyze them. You decide that you should sort the data alphabetically by the substance and the concentration of each substance. Filtering the results for the substances where you had significant amounts of fermentation will also aid you in deciding what were good substrates for yeast.

a. Create a custom sort on the Fermentation Data Table worksheet, where the first-level sort is by Substance in A–Z order and the second level is by Concentration in Smallest to Largest order.

b. Filter the data to display only the following substances: **Ethanol**, **NaCl**, and **Sucrose**.

c. Add a new field to the right of the 65 minute field. Rename the new field **Good for Fermentation**, apply Wrap Text to the cell, and then change the column width to 15.

d. Create a formula with a structured reference, using the IF function, that determines if the amount of CO_2 production at 65 minutes is greater than or equal to 2.0; if so, it will display the word *Yes*; otherwise, it will display the word *No*.

Apply Conditional Formatting

To highlight the values at certain intervals, you decide to apply conditional formatting to illustrate the differences.

a. Apply the **Orange Data Bar** conditional formatting in the Gradient Fill section to the 30 minute interval.

b. Apply the **Green Data Bar** conditional formatting in the Gradient Fill section to the 45 minute interval.

c. Apply the **Highlight Cells Rules, Greater Than** conditional formatting to the 60 minute interval, where values greater than 1.5 are formatted with **Light Red Fill with Dark Red Text**.

d. Create a new conditional format that applies bold red font where the values equal *Yes* in the Good for Fermentation column.

e. Select the **Good for Fermentation column** and center the data.

f. Select and center all of the column headings.

Create a Line Chart

The results for salt (NaCl) are interesting in that you would not have expected salt at any concentration to be good for yeast fermentation. You know that sugar is added to bread dough to stimulate the yeast's ability to raise the dough. At differing concentrations for each substrate, it appears that it does make a difference in the amount of CO_2 created, as indicated by the rise in volume in the pipette. You have isolated the results for NaCl and decide to create a line chart to visualize the changes over time.

a. Select the **range A5:N9** on the NaCl worksheet. Create a line chart.

b. Move the chart to its own sheet and name it **Line Chart**. Move it to the right of the Fermentation Data Table worksheet.

c. Apply Layout 4 from the Quick Layout gallery.

d. Insert the chart title: **NaCl Concentration Evaluation**.

e. Add axis titles: **Minutes** on the primary horizontal axis and **Volume (mL)** on the primary vertical axis.

f. Move the legend to the right.

Finalize the Workbook

You want to prepare the fermentation lab workbook in case someone wants to print any of the worksheets. To ensure that each worksheet prints only on one page, you need to adjust the page setup options.

a. Create a footer on each worksheet with your name, the sheet name code, and the file name code.

b. Apply landscape orientation to the **NaCl** worksheet. Change the scaling so that all the columns fit on one page and the gridlines will print.

c. Apply landscape orientation to the **Fermentation Data Table** worksheet. Change the scaling so the sheet fits on one page.

d. Save and close the workbook. Based on your instructor's directions, submit the following:

   04e_DensityLab_LastFirst

   04e_FermentationLab_LastFirst

Science Professionals

Use Microsoft Access

Background

Databases are an important tool in assisting scientists as a way of storing and analyzing data collected from scientific experiments and published literature. Microsoft Access can be used to create and maintain tables, create and edit queries, and create forms and reports.

Skills:

Chapter 1

Open a Database, Save a Database, Enable Content in a Database, Explore Table Datasheet View, Sort Table Data, Change Data in Table Datasheet View, Explore Table Design View, Add Records to a Table, Use Filter by Form, Use a Selection Filter to Find Exact Matches, Compact and Repair a Database, Backup a Database

Chapter 2

Work with Field Properties, Create a Table in Design View, Set a Table's Primary Key, Modify a Table in Datasheet View, Modify a Table in Design View, Import Excel Data, Establish Table Relationships, Enforce Referential Integrity, Create a Table in Datasheet View, Create a Single Table Query in Design View, Specify Query Criteria, Create a Multi-table Query, Modify a Multi-table Query, Run, Copy and Modify a Query

Chapter 3

Display a Totals Row in a Table, Create a Calculated Field in a Query, Format Fields in a Query, Use the Expression Builder, Use the IIf Function, Create a Totals Query, Display a Total Row for a Query, Format Fields in a Report

Chapter 4

Create a Form Using the Form Tool, Use Form Views, Format Controls, Enter Data in Form View, Create Reports Using the Report Wizard, Sort Records in a Report, Remove a Field from a Report, Modify Column Widths in a Report

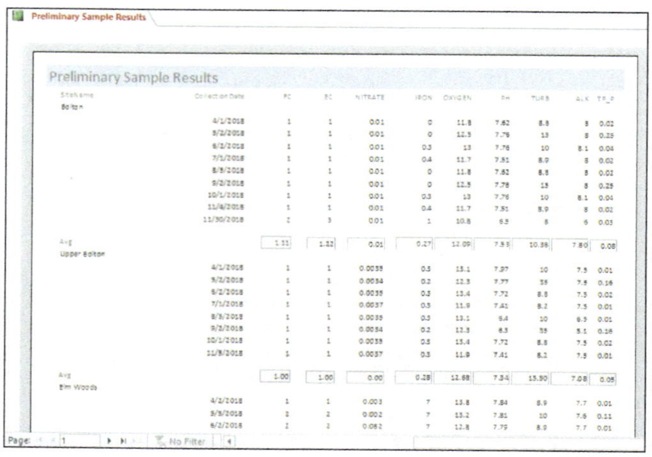

Access 2016, Windows 10, Microsoft Corporation

FIGURE 4.3 Working as a Science Professional Database Table

CASE STUDY | Working as a Science Professional

Starting Files	Files to be Submitted
04a_GroveCreek	**04a_GroveCreek_LastFirst**
04a_CreekSampleResults.xlsx	**04a_GroveCreek_LastFirst_CurrentDate**

Capstone Exercises

You have a work–study job as a laboratory assistant in the biology department. The professor has been assessing the health of the Grove Run Creek that flows into Lake Wellburk. Students have been collecting water and aquatic life samples from April through November to check chemical and biological indicators. The water samples have been analyzed by a local testing facility, and students have identified the aquatic organisms. A database has already been created to store the collected data on the water samples. You have been asked to review the data and set up the database so that more data can be entered and manipulated easily. You will create and edit tables, queries, forms, and reports. The data from the testing facility is in an Excel file, and you will import that data into your Access database.

Use the Existing Database

After reviewing the data that was collected and with input from the professor about what information will be expected for reports, you are ready to review the database currently in use.

a. Open the database as *04a_GroveCreek* and save it as **04a_GroveCreek_LastFirst**. Enable Content.
b. Open the *Samples* table and examine the data.
c. Sort the Samples table in ascending order by the SiteID field.
d. Click **Save** on the Quick Access toolbar to save the sort to the table.
e. Make a correction for the record with the SampleID of S00002. The StudentID is incorrect. Change the StudentID from 010225 to 034889.
f. Switch to Design view and change the field size for SampleID to **6** and the StudentID field size to **6**.
g. Format the CollectionDate field to **Short Date**.
h. Save the table. Click **Yes** in the warning dialog box to continue, as the existing data will not be lost due to formatting the Collection Date field. Close the table.

Create the Sites Table

You need to create a table to store the names and locations of the sites where the samples were collected.

a. Create a new table in Design View.
b. Create a **SiteID** field that will function as the primary key, with a data type of **Short Text** and a field size of **3**.
c. Add a second field named **SiteName** with data type as **Short Text** and a field size of **25**.
d. Add a third field named **Location**. It will have a data type of **Short Text** and a field size of **50**.

e. Save the table with the name **Sites**. Enter the records into the new table:

SiteID	SiteName	Location
C01	Bolton	Route 29 South Marker 10
C02	Upper Bolton	Route 118 West Marker 20
C03	Elm Woods	Elm Road Marker 30
C04	Smith Farm	Smith Farm Road Marker 40
C05	Overbrook	Daisy Lane Marker 50

f. Adjust the column widths to Best Fit.

g. Save and close the table.

Create the Researcher Table

You need to create a table to store the names of the students who collected the samples.

a. Create a new table.

b. Add field names and data types as listed next. Adjust the field properties accordingly:

Field Name	Data Type	Field Properties	
StudentID	Short Text	Field Size: 6	
FirstName	Short Text	Field Size: 20	Caption: First Name
LastName	Short Text	Field Size: 25	Caption: Last Name
Experience	Yes/No		

c. Set the **StudentID field** as the primary key.

d. Save the table with the name **Researcher**.

e. Enter the records into the new table:

StudentID	First Name	Last Name	Experience
010225	Michael	Geisinger	Yes
023311	Diana	Shroyer	No
034562	Robert	Barry	Yes
034889	James	King	No
040254	Addyson	Burkley	Yes
054321	Your First Name	Your Last Name	No

f. Close the table.

Share Data with Excel

The table that stores the sample results, Samples, is missing the data for July through November. The data was recorded in an Excel spreadsheet by the previous work–study student. You now need to bring the data into the Access database, adding the data to the existing Samples table.

a. Append the data of the *04a_CreekSampleResults* Excel file to the Samples table.

b. Open the Samples table and examine the data.

c. Verify the number of samples. There should be a total of 40 records.

d. Close the table.

Establish Table Relationships

Now that all of the tables have been designed and populated, it is time to create relationships between the tables so you can extract the data efficiently. You will set the relationships and enforce referential integrity.

a. Add all of the tables to the Relationships window and close the Show Table window.

b. Create a relationship between the Researcher table and the Samples table by dragging the **StudentID** field in the Researcher table onto the **StudentID** field in the Samples table. Enforce referential integrity.

c. Create a relationship between the Sites table and the Samples table by dragging the **SiteID** field in the Sites table onto the **SiteID** field in the Samples table. Enforce referential integrity.

d. Save and close the Relationships window.

Create a Form Using a Form Tool

You need to create a form to enter additional sample data that will be collected for Part 2 of the project. The quickest way to create a form is to select a table and then use the Form Tool.

a. Create a form based on the Samples table.

b. Change the title label to **Streams Entering Lake Wellburk Sample Results.**

c. Reduce the size of the text box controls to approximately **2"** wide.

d. Select the labels, apply bold formatting, and then change the font color to **Dark Blue** (under Standard Colors).

e. Add the following new record:

SampleID	S00041
SiteID	C01
StudentID	054321
CollectionDate	11/30/2018
FC	2
EC	3
NITRATE	0.01
IRON	1
OXYGEN	10.8
PH	6.5
TURB	8
ALK	6
TP_P	0.03

f. Save the form as **Sample Testing Results** and close the form.

Create Filters

You need to quickly identify all of the samples collected after April 1, 2018, where the EC count is greater than 1. High EC counts are known to be an issue with drinking-water quality.

a. Open the Samples table.

b. Use Filter by Form to filter the records to find all of the samples collected after 4/1/2018 with EC > 1.

c. Apply the filter. Copy the resulting records. Create a new blank table in Datasheet view. Click Paste, and choose Paste Append, to add them into a new table. Save the table as **HighEC**.
d. Add a Totals row to the HighEC table. Display the maximum FC and the minimum EC values.
e. Apply a Filter by Selection to the HighEC table where SiteID equals C04.
f. Save and close the HighEC table.
g. Close the Samples table and do not save the changes.

Create Single-Table Queries

You need to create a query to analyze all of the samples collected in July 2018 and a query to display all samples where the pH is less than 6.5.

a. Create a query. Include all fields from the Samples table.
b. Add criteria to show all records where the collection date is between 7/1/2018 and 7/31/2018.
c. Run the query. Save the query as **July 2018 Samples**.
d. Verify that the results are only from July. Close the query.
e. Create a query. Include the SampleID, SiteID, and PH fields from the Samples table.
f. Add criteria to show all records where the PH field is less than 6.5.
g. Run the query. Save the query as **Unacceptable PH Samples**.
h. Review the results and close the query.

Create a Multi-Table Query

You need to create a query to see if there is any correlation to some of the sample result differences due to inexperienced students collecting the samples.

a. Create a query using the Researcher, Samples, and Sites tables.
b. Add the SampleID field from the Samples table; the SiteName and Location from the Sites table; and the FirstName, LastName, and Experience fields from the Researcher table. Then, from the Samples table, add in the CollectionDate, FC, and PH fields.
c. Add criteria to display only those records from students with no experience.
d. Run the query and save the query as **Samples Collected by Inexperienced Students**. Close the query.

Create a Calculated Field in a Query

The bacterial counts can be combined for analysis. You need to create a query that adds the FC and EC counts together for each sample.

a. Create a query using the Samples table; include the SampleID, SiteID, CollectionDate, FC, and EC fields.
b. Save the query as **Total Coliforms Count**.
c. Create a calculated field in the first blank column in the query design grid named TotalColiforms that adds the FC and EC fields together.
d. Format the caption for the calculated field to **Total Coliform Count**.
e. Run the query. Check to see that the calculated field has correctly added the FC and EC fields. Adjust all fields to Best Fit.
f. Return to Design view and do not display the FC and EC fields. Save and close the query.

Use Functions in a Query

To make some of the data easier for review, you will create a calculated field to display "Acceptable" or "Unacceptable" for samples where the water meets drinking standards for iron content.

a. Create a query using the Samples table; include SampleID, SiteID, and CollectionDate fields from the Samples table.
b. Use the Expression Builder to create a field called **IronMCL**, using the IIf function, in the first blank column in the query design grid. The string "Acceptable" will be applied if the iron value is <= 0.3; otherwise, the string "Unacceptable" will be applied.
c. Run the query. Save the query as **Iron Maximum Contaminant Levels**.
d. Copy the Iron Maximum Contaminant Levels query and save it as **Unacceptable Iron Contaminant Levels**.
e. Apply a filter to view only those records that are unacceptable.
f. Save the filter and close the query.

Create a Totals Query

You need to analyze all of the sample testing data by site to arrive at the Average, Minimum, and Maximum counts for some of the tests performed.

a. Create a query using the Sites and Samples tables; include SiteName from the Sites table, and the OXYGEN, TURB, and TP_P fields from the Samples table.
b. Display the Total row. Calculate the average OXYGEN, minimum TURB, and maximum TP_P.
c. Change the format for AvgofOXYGEN to Fixed.
d. Run the query. Save the query as **Oxygen, Turbidity, and Phosphorus Results by Site**.
e. Close the query.

Create a Report Using the Report Wizard

The professor has asked you to create a report representing the sample results by site so a decision can be made on further sample testing.

a. Use the Report Wizard to create a report. Select SiteName from the Sites table. Select all of the fields from the Samples table except SampleID, SiteID, and StudentID.
b. Accept the defaults for Grouping. Sort in ascending order by CollectionDate.
c. Add Summary options, showing Detail and Summary, and select Avg for all fields listed.
d. Choose the **Stepped Layout** and the **Landscape** orientation.
e. Save the Report as **Preliminary Sample Results**.
f. Change the Format property of the TP_P field to **Fixed**.
g. Change the Format property of all of the Avg field text boxes to **Fixed**.
h. Modify any labels and text boxes to keep the fields nicely spaced and all data visible.
i. Delete the Summary for "SiteID" control in the SiteID footer.
j. View the report in Report view to make sure it will display on one page only. View in Print Preview and it should be two pages in length. Save and close the report.

Compact, Repair, and Back Up the Database

To make sure that your database operates efficiently and securely, you are going to compact the database and create a duplicate copy of your database as a backup.

a. Compact and repair the database.

b. Back up the database in the location where you save your student files. Accept the default file name (adds the current date to the file name) and save it.

c. Close the database and exit Access.

d. Based on your instructor's directions, submit the following files:

   04a_GroveCreek_LastFirst

   04a_GroveCreek_LastFirst_CurrentDate

Science Professionals

Use Microsoft PowerPoint

Background

College students majoring in the sciences will often be required to present the results of their findings. Microsoft PowerPoint makes it possible to create presentations with media objects, charts, transitions, and animations to aid in delivering results to an audience. Being able to communicate one's work visually using Microsoft PowerPoint is a necessary skill.

Skills:

Chapter 1

Insert a Header and Footer, Insert a Table, Modify a Table, Apply Transitions, Animate Objects, Run a Slideshow

Chapter 2

Create a New Presentation, Reuse Slides, Use Sections, Modify a Slide Master

Chapter 3

Create WordArt, Modify WordArt, Convert Text to SmartArt, Modify SmartArt, Create SmartArt, Create and Modify a Shape

Chapter 4

Apply and Modify a Theme, Insert an Online Picture, Insert a Picture from File, Apply a Picture Style, Add Audio from File, Change Audio Settings

New

Use Start Inking

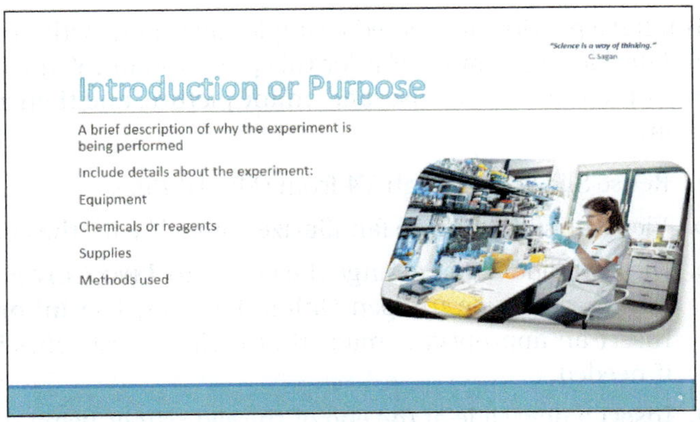

FIGURE 4.4 Working as a Science Professional Presentation

CASE STUDY | Working as a Science Professional

Starting Files	Files to be Submitted
04p_Writing	**04p_Guidelines_LastFirst**
04p_Scientist.jpg	
04p_Music.mid	
04p_Quote.jpg	

Capstone Exercises

It is important that science majors are knowledgeable in creating their laboratory and scientific reports. Because you have written several successful reports, your instructor has asked you to prepare a slideshow in PowerPoint and present it to several classes. Your slideshow will cover the key points of writing scientific reports and of data usage. Your instructor has asked that you include charts, images, and audio to enhance the presentation.

Create a New Presentation

You create a title slide for the new presentation, apply a theme, and create a Notes and Handouts header and footer.

a. Create a new blank PowerPoint presentation and save it as **04p_Guidelines_LastFirst**.
b. Enter the following text in the placeholders of the Title slide:
   - Title placeholder: **Guide to Writing Scientific Laboratory Reports**
   - In the Subtitle placeholder, type your name.
c. Create a Notes and Handouts header with your name and a handout footer with **Guidelines**. Include the date and time, updated automatically. Apply to all.
d. Apply the **Retrospect** theme.
e. Change the color of the theme to **Blue Green**.

Add Existing Content to the Presentation

You have previously created a simple slide show with no formatting for this assignment and decide to use most of it for this presentation. You will add these slides to your existing presentation first, insert an online picture, and then add a new slide to the end of the show.

a. Reuse Slides 2 through 14 from *04p_Writing.*
b. View the slide show to familiarize yourself with the contents.
c. Display Slide 2 and change the layout to **Two Content.** Use the content placeholder on the right side to open Online Pictures. Use **laboratory** as the search keyword. Insert an appropriate image that includes test tubes into the placeholder and resize if needed.
d. Insert a new slide at the end of the slide show, using the **Blank** layout.
e. Insert WordArt. Select **Fill: Black, Text color 1; Outline: White, - Background color 1; Hard Shadow: White, - Background color 1** and type **Any Questions?**
f. Format the WordArt, using the Text Effect **Glow: 18 point; Teal, Accent color 3**.
g. Copy the Online Picture of a laboratory used on Slide 2 and position the image in the lower-right portion of your slide and size it appropriately.

Insert a Table

To demonstrate what a data table should look like, you decide to include one in the presentation.

a. Change the layout of Slide 14 (*Tables*) to the **Two Content** layout.

b. Insert a table with three columns and five rows into the placeholder on the right and type the data shown below.

Sample	Volume (mL)	Mass (g)
1	6.0	17.20
2	7.0	17.76
3	6.2	17.08
4	7.2	18.06

c. Center the column titles and the column with the sample numbers.

d. Right align the values for the volume and mass of samples 1–4.

e. Select table and change the font size to **24 pt**.

f. Resize the table to a height of **4″** and a width of **5.5″**.

Create SmartArt and Add a Shape

You decide that the presentation would be more interesting if you used SmartArt features to add visual appeal to some of the slides.

a. Display Slide 4 and convert the bulleted list to SmartArt, choosing **Vertical Box List** as the SmartArt layout.

b. Change the colors of the SmartArt image to **Colorful - Accent Colors**.

c. Apply the SmartArt style **Polished**.

d. Display Slide 3 and select the placeholder **Insert a SmartArt Graphic**.

e. Choose **Circle Process**. Type **Introduction** in the first shape. Type **Methods and Materials** in the second shape. Type **Results** in the third shape.

f. Add an additional shape after *Results* and type **Discussion**.

g. Apply the SmartArt style **Intense Effect**.

h. Display Slide 10. Create a **Cloud Callout** shape.

i. In the callout type, **What is the specific purpose of this study?** Format the callout style to **Colored Fill - Teal, Accent 3**. Increase the font size to **20 pt**.

j. Resize the callout to a height of **2.3″** and width of **3″**.

k. Position the callout to the middle of the right side of your slide. Move the pointer part of the callout to point to the sentence on the slide that begins with *Be specific*.

l. Display Slide 12 and convert the bullet list to SmartArt, choosing **Hierarchy List** as your SmartArt layout.

m. Change the color of the SmartArt image to **Dark 2 Fill**.

Inserting Images and Audio

Your slideshow needs a good ending to further enhance the presentation. You decide to add a lab-related photo and an audio file to add interest also.

a. Display Slide 9 (*Introduction or Purpose*), and change the slide layout to **Two Content**.

b. Add an image to the right content placeholder by inserting the picture *04p_Scientist.jpg*.

c. Apply the Picture Style **Bevel Perspective** to the picture.

d. Display the last slide in the slide show (*Any Questions?*) and insert an audio file, using the option Audio on My PC. Select the file *04p_Music.mid*. Set it to **Start Automatically, Loop until Stopped** and **Hide During Show.**
e. Position the sound icon to the bottom-left corner of the slide.

Create Sections and Move a Section

As you review your presentation, you realize you could benefit from organizing your slides into sections and modify the outline structure by moving a section to another area of your slide show.

a. Add a section named **Format** between Slides 2 and 3.
b. Add a section named **Guidelines** between Slides 6 and 7.
c. Add a section named **Structure** between Slides 8 and 9.
d. Add a section named **Help** between Slides 14 and 15.
e. Switch to Slide Sorter view. Move the **Guidelines** section above the **Format** section.
f. Return to Normal View.

Modify the Slide Master

You want to change the font for the titles on each slide to a WordArt style. You also want to add an inspirational quote that will appear on all of the slides. You will customize the presentation by using the Slide Master.

a. View the Slide Master.
b. Click the slide master at the top of the list.
c. Select the placeholder **Click to edit Master title style**, and apply the WordArt style **Fill: Aqua, Accent color 2; Outline: Aqua, Accent color 2**.
d. Add an image to the top right corner by inserting the picture *04p_Quote.jpg.*
e. Save the changes and close Master View.
f. View the slideshow.

Finalize the Presentation

You are now ready to add interest to the presentation by adding animations and applying a transition effect to the slides. After viewing the presentation, you decide to use the Start Inking feature to highlight some concepts.

a. Select the bullet placeholder on Slide 2, apply the **Underline** animation, and then set the animation to start After Previous.
b. Select the SmartArt on Slide 5 and apply the **Grow & Turn** animation. Apply the **One by One** effect option.
c. Select the SmartArt on Slide 6 and apply the **Float In** animation. Apply the **Level One by One** effect option.
d. Apply the **Switch** transition to all slides.
e. Display Slide 7. On the Review tab, select **Start Inking**. Choose the **Aqua Highlighter**, and apply the highlighter to the text **Materials and Equipment** and **Materials and Methods**.
f. Select **Stop Inking**.
g. View the presentation.
h. Save and close the file. Based on your instructor's directions, submit **04p_Guidelines_LastFirst**

Science Professionals

Integrate Microsoft Office Programs

Background

When it comes to using Microsoft Office, many Office programs can accomplish the same basic task, but knowing which one is best suited for a particular project is important. It is important to think about what the result should look like, how complicated it will be to get there, and what features are needed to accomplish the goal. Microsoft Word is best utilized when creating lab and scientific reports. Microsoft Excel is utilized for charting and calculating data. Microsoft Access is the best choice for managing large amounts of data that have been collected and when queries and reports need to be generated. Microsoft PowerPoint is valuable for creating presentations to report experimental findings and explain scientific principles. At times, several programs are used to create a final document or report, as needed to create the desired results.

Skills:

Create Charts from Excel Data, Paste Excel Worksheets or Charts into a Word Document, Import Data from Access and Excel into an Access database, Create Queries with Calculated Fields, Create and Modify a Report in Access, Format a Document, Use Mail Merge

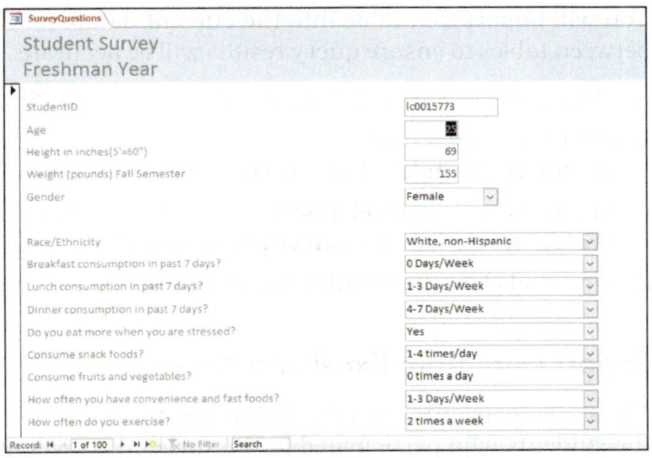

Access 2016, Windows 10, Microsoft Corporation

FIGURE 4.5 Working as a Science Professional Database Form

CASE STUDY | Working as a Science Professional

Starting Files	Files to be Submitted
04i_Survey.accdb	**04i_Survey_LastFirst.accdb**
04i_SpringResults.accdb	**04i_SurveyStatistics_LastFirst.xlsx**
04i_WeightChange.docx	**04i_WeightChange_LastFirst.docx**
04i_ThankYou.docx	**04i_Merged_LastFirst.docx**
04i_SurveyAddresses.xlsx	

Capstone Exercises

You are working as a lab assistant in the biology department at your school, where you, several other students, and the professor have been collaborating on a research project they are hoping to publish. The project consists of a survey that was developed and completed by student volunteers to assess weight gain and behavioral patterns during college that may contribute to excessive weight gain and obesity in later life.

The data was collected using Access, and the initial observations were obtained by applying filters to the results of the survey table. By exporting the survey results into Excel, it may be easier to use some of its features for the statistics. You need to create some queries in an Access database to analyze the rest of the data. The research report has been written, but is not complete. You need to make some changes to the report and create some charts. You have also been asked to send out a thank-you letter along with a gift card to the students who completed the survey, and will create a mail merge to facilitate sending them.

Import Data from an Access Database

Measurements of student height and weight were obtained in the fall semester. At the end of the spring semester, all students were weighed again. The initial results from the fall semester were entered in a table in an Access database created by another student. You will import that table into the current database. You need to create a relationship between tables to ensure query results will be accurate.

a. Open the *04i_Survey* database and save it as **04i_Survey_LastFirst**. Enable content.
b. Import external data from Access, using the *04i_SpringResults* database, importing the **SpringWeighIn** table. Do not save the import steps.
c. Create a one-to-one relationship and enforce referential integrity between the **SpringWeighIn** table and the **SurveyResults** table.
d. Save and close the Relationships window.

Import Data from Excel into Access

The student government association has provided you with the names and addresses of the students who participated in the survey. You will import them into the database to keep all of the data for the survey in one place and to be able to send the students a thank-you letter. You need to create a relationship between the tables in the database.

a. Using the *04i_SurveyAddresses* workbook, import external data from Excel into a new table in the current database. Indicate that the first row contains column headings, with StudentID as the primary key, and accept Addresses as the table name. Do not save the import steps.
b. Create a one-to-one relationship and enforce referential integrity between the **Addresses** table and the **SurveyResults** table.
c. Save and close the Relationships window.

Create Queries with Calculated Fields

The only query that has been done determines the body mass index (BMI) at the beginning of the fall semester. Now, you need to create additional queries about BMI and weight gain.

a. Create a query to determine the BMI for the end of the spring semester. Include the StudentID and Weight2 fields from the SpringWeighIn table and the Height field from the SurveyResults table. Create a calculated field for the body mass index; by typing **FinalBMI: Weight2*703/(Height*Height)**.

b. Format the FinalBMI field to Fixed and display only two decimals. Do not display the Height field. Save the query as **FinalBMI**, and then close it.

c. Create a query to determine the amount of weight gain per student. Include the StudentID and Weight1 fields from the SurveyResults table and the Weight2 field from the SpringWeighIn table. Create a calculated field named **WeightGain** that calculates the difference between the Weight2 and Weight1 fields.

d. Run the query. Add a Total row to the datasheet and determine the average weight gain. Save the query as **WeightGainPerStudent**.

e. Copy the WeightGainPerStudent query and save it as **EatingHabits**.

f. Add fields to the EatingHabits query. Using the SurveyResults table, add the following fields: Q01, Q02, Q03, Q04, Q05, Q06, and Q07. Do not display the Weight1 and Weight2 fields.

g. Run the query. Use Filter by Selection to display records where WeightGain is not equal to 0. Change the Total row for the WeightGain field to Count.

h. Save and close the query.

Create a Report

The advisor for the research project asked you to create a report in Access to display the eating habits of the students who gained weight, especially how many times a day they consume snack foods, exercise, and spend time watching TV or using the computer.

a. Use the Report Wizard to create the report, selecting the WeightGain field from the WeightGainPerStudent query and the Q04, Q08, and Q12 fields from the SurveyResults table.

b. Accept all of the default settings except for the lay out. Select Landscape orientation and save the report as **Weight Gain Analysis**.

c. Modify the report so that the labels and text boxes are nicely spaced and all data and labels are visible.

d. Apply conditional formatting for the WeightGain field to display values greater than 5, with the font color Red (standard color).

e. Save and close the report.

Import Data in Excel and Create a Chart

A worksheet with statistics needs to be created, and you decide to export the data from Access into Excel. You need to create another query first and will then export the query to Excel and use the data to create a chart. Additional data to create another chart needs to be entered into Excel.

a. Create a query using the Simple Query Wizard. Select the **Gender field** from the SurveyResults table, the BMI field from the InitialBMI query, and the FinalBMI field from the FinalBMI query.

b. Select **Summary** and choose **Summary Options**, selecting Avg for both BMI fields. Save the query as **BMIComparison** and select the option to modify the query.

c. Change the caption for the Avg of BMI field to **Avg Initial BMI** and change the caption for the Avg of FinalBMI field to **Avg Final BMI**. Run the query and adjust the column widths so the field names are visible.

d. Export the BMIComparison query into Excel. Save the workbook and name it **04i_SurveyStatistics_LastFirst.xlsx**.

e. Export the data with formatting and layout, and open the destination file after the export operation is complete. Do not save the export steps. Close Access.

f. Select **the range A1:C3** of the BMIComparison worksheet and create a clustered column chart. Change the chart title to **All Students by Gender**. Move the chart directly under the data.

g. Insert a new worksheet and name it **Exercise**. Enter the following text and data into the worksheet starting at **cell A3**. Widen columns so all data is displayed.

Exercise Type	Female	Male
Aerobic Exercise (3 or more times/week)	11	8
Stretching (2–3 times/week)	5	9
Strength training (2–3 times/week)	2	12
At least one of the above	26	18
No exercise	20	20

h. Select the **range A3:C8** and create a clustered column chart. Title the chart **Exercise Type by Gender**. Move the chart directly under the data.

i. Save the workbook. Keep the workbook open.

Format the Document and Insert the Charts

The research report is still a work in progress. You need to insert a watermark so it is not accidentally released before it is reviewed by everyone. It is also missing page numbers, and the footnotes need to be converted to endnotes. You also need to insert the charts you created in Excel into the report before you pass it along for further review and completion.

a. Open the *04i_WeightChange.docx* file and save it as **04i_WeightChange_LastFirst**.

b. Insert a custom diagonal watermark, with the text **For Review Only**, and change the font color to Red.

c. Insert a page number at the bottom of the page, using the **Bold Numbers 2** style.

d. Click the **References tab** and open the Footnotes dialog box in the Footnotes group. Convert the footnotes to endnotes.

e. Insert the **All Students by Gender** chart from the BMIComparison worksheet to page 4 under the heading *GRAPH 1: BMI Comparison*, using Paste Special to paste it as a Microsoft Excel Chart Object.

f. Insert the **Exercise Type by Gender** chart from the Exercise worksheet under the heading *GRAPH 2: EXERCISE Comparison* (top of page 5), using Paste Special to paste it as a Microsoft Excel Chart Object.

g. Save and close the document.

h. Save and close the workbook.

Create a Mail Merge to Send Out Letters

You created a thank-you letter to send to the survey participants and are now ready to make the final formatting changes and complete a mail merge. You will save the mail-merged letters for printing on school letterhead and mailing next week when the gift cards are sent over from the student government coordinator.

a. Open the *04i_ThankYou.docx* file.

b. Start mail merge by using the Step-by-Step Mail Merge Wizard to select the Letters mail merge process.

c. Use the current document to start the letter.

d. Select recipients, using an existing list, from the Addresses table in the *04i_Survey_LastFirst* database. Refine the recipient list by sorting it by LastName in ascending order.

e. Insert an address block using the default form of *Joshua Randall Jr.* as the recipient name and accept the other defaults.

f. Press Enter twice and insert a greeting line in the form of *Dear Joshua:*

g. Preview your letters to verify the address block and greeting lines are correct.

h. Complete the merge step but do not print any of the documents (you would have 100 letters). Save the merged letter file as **04i_Merged_LastFirst** and close the document.

i. Close the *04i_ThankYou* document and do not save it.

j. Based on your instructor's directions, submit the following files:

   04i_Survey_LastFirst.accdb

   04i_SurveyStatistics_LastFirst.xlsx

   04i_WeightChange_LastFirst.docx

   04i_Merged_LastFirst.docx